What Are You Waiting For?

What Are You Waiting For?

A practical guide to

knowing what you want

and making it happen ...

SHELLEY BRUNSKILL-MATSON

First published 2015

Exisle Publishing Limited,
P.O. Box 60-490, Titirangi, Auckland 0642, New Zealand.
'Moonrising', Narone Creek Road, Wollombi, NSW 2325, Australia.
www.exislepublishing.com

A catalogue record for this book is available from
the National Library of New Zealand.

ISBN 978-1-921966-65-1

10 9 8 7 6 5 4 3 2 1

Text design and production by IslandBridge
Cover design by www.CVdesign.net.nz
Printed in Shenzhen, China, by Ink Asia

Contents

This book is for you.

You inspire me and make me a better person
simply by being in my life, and being you.
I love you.

(What is special is that I know I needn't
name you individually for you to know
this is for you.)

Acknowledgements

First I want to thank my incredibly special husband Paul, without whom none of this would have been possible. You have believed in me and been there for me every step of the way, not only as I've written this book but since the first day we met. You are a truly amazing man. You are my rock.

A huge thanks also to my four gorgeous children, Alex, Andre, Brooke and Carley. Thank you for keeping me real, reminding me daily what matters most in life and for inspiring me to want to be a better person. I am as blessed and proud as any mother could be.

I wish to thank my parents. I thank my late father, Tony, for inspiring me to live life fully. It is because of you that I am determined to make such a dent in this world. To my mother, Lynn, thank you for your unconditional love and support. You are a strong and courageous woman.

Thank you also to my sister Christina and my Aunty Jill. Christina, thank you for holding my hand in a way no one else can. I am incredibly proud of you. Jill, thank you for your unwavering support and encouragement. You are the most positive person I know, and such a special part of my life.

I also extend a heartfelt thanks to my wonderful clients, who so generously let me walk alongside them. Thank you for letting me into your lives as you do. You are incredible, every one of you. Your courage and determination to be your best is truly inspiring.

Thank you also to Sue Reidy of Sue Reidy Communications — the first person to ever read my manuscript. Your feedback, encouragement and advice were exactly what I needed. You were more pivotal in this book getting to market than I am sure you will ever give yourself credit for. A big thank you to Geoff Walker of Geoff Walker Publishing for your words of encouragement and voice of experience, too. It gave me great confidence having you in my corner.

Finally, thank you, wholeheartedly, to Gareth St John Thomas, Ian Watt and the team at Exisle Publishing for seeing the potential in this book and being willing to give an unpublished author a go. You have been fantastic to work with.

Introduction
About this book

Is your life just as you want it? Are you 'living your dream'? Or are you waiting for some future event or point in time (maybe once the kids are older or when you have more money, more time or more ...), when you will *then* be able to start living the life you want?

As a Life Coach and busy mother of four, I meet a lot of people from all walks of life. Over recent years I have become increasingly aware of the number of conversations (both in work and in social situations) in which people talk about what they will do or have 'one day' or 'once ...'. When talking about what they want for themselves, people tend to change the tense in which they are speaking. What may begin as a conversation about what they want for themselves now, in the present day, suddenly becomes a future-based conversation. It is as though people struggle to consider that they could actually have what they want for themselves, in the present, today. Instead, there is always a 'something' that has to happen first, a reason why they have to wait. This is a trend I have spent much of the last few years observing and studying.

I believe that most people are capable of achieving and experiencing so much more in life than they ever do. Few people, too few, actually live their lives as fully, or as fully contented, as they could. To a greater or lesser extent, the majority of people live 'safe', 'risk-free' lives. They live passively, rather than proactively. They may dream of what it is they want, but never dare 'put themselves out there' to make it happen. Instead, they create 'valid reasons' why they 'can't, not yet', why they *have to* wait. Others have no idea what it is that they want for themselves. Yet they typically do little to clarify their wants, 'waiting' too, waiting to know what they want.

The world over, people wait. It's uncomfortable to step outside one's comfort zone. So what happens? Nothing. Too many people unknowingly allow themselves to be paralysed by their fear. Fear that never subsides.

The majority of people spend their entire lives waiting to live the lives they wish they could live.

Purpose

I am writing this book because I want to change this. I want to challenge society's acceptance of what I see as a 'waiting epidemic'. I want to be a catalyst for people to stop bullshitting themselves and to start living the lives they're waiting to live. Not 'one day', not 'once ...' or 'when ...', but effective immediately.

My message is simple: 'Stop waiting to live. Become clear about what you want, make it big, make it matter and make it happen.'

Why am I so passionate about this? Because I know what is possible.

I spent many years waiting to live the life I wanted. Among other things, I waited to do work I felt truly mattered. I waited to be part of a relationship in which I could fully be myself. I waited to pursue my love of dancing. It was only when I woke up to the realisation that if I was to have these things in my life, it was up to me to make them happen, that I truly started living my life.

This book is written to enable you to do so as well.

NOT 'just another motivational book'!

Walk into any bookshop and you will find the self-help section saturated with motivational reads. This book is different. This book is highly practical. From my point of view, it has to be. What benefit would there be in writing a book aimed at inspiring readers to become clear about what they want in their lives, and to make it happen, if it didn't also show you *how* to do so?

You will see that a portion of the book is shaded. This section, Chapters 7 to 12 inclusive, takes you through my comprehensive five-step process to help you to clarify what you want in life. Those of you who may already have a clear view of what it is you want may be tempted to skip over this section. That is your prerogative, of course. Read the first six chapters and then continue reading from Chapter 13. That said, I am confident that even the most 'sorted' of people will benefit from the exercises Chapters 7 to 12 contain. Who knows what else you might learn about yourself?

As well as being cram-packed with practical tools and strategies, this book also includes my favourite motivational quotes — to inspire you, and my pick of the most powerful coaching questions — to challenge you. As a coach I am a great believer in the power of fabulous questions to help one access one's thoughts. I also encourage you to take the time to fully consider the Reflective Questions at the end of each (non-shaded) chapter.

I say it as it is

It matters to me that this book 'says it as it is'. I am not one to mince my words (as you may already have noticed). I won't 'soften' my message to make it more palatable, as I can't risk my message being lost or diluted.

It is also no accident that this is a 'quick pick up and read'. There are so many self-help books out there — too many of them, in my view — filled with pages of unnecessary words. This book needs to be reader-friendly. We are all busy. It makes no sense for me to write a 400-page book when my message can be communicated far more succinctly. With this in mind, I have very consciously kept my words to a minimum, for both of our sakes!

Warning – I hope to make you feel uncomfortable!

Throughout this book I ask you to consider questions we don't like to ask ourselves. Questions that inevitably make us feel uncomfortable, even defensive, because they cause us to question the very thoughts that allow us to feel okay about where we are in life. In doing so, at some level, such questions challenge the very core of who we are. However, they need to be asked — and you owe it to yourself to be honest in answering them. For some of you, this book may not teach you anything new, but it may remind you of what you already know. For others it will, I hope, make your current approach to life, your current choices, no longer acceptable to you.

Write it down

I encourage you to have pen and paper (perhaps an exercise book or a journal) at hand while reading this book. Or open a new file and record your thoughts electronically, if that will work better for you. Whatever medium you choose, recording your responses to the questions asked is an important step in helping you process and clarify your thoughts. There is something about writing down your thoughts that allows you to see them more clearly. Simply reading through the exercises will not have the same effect. Your brain is for *having* ideas, not holding them. Write down whatever comes to mind. Refrain from editing your responses — just record them as they occur to you. And be completely honest with yourself. No one else need be privy to what you write (unless of course you choose to share your workings).

No serial self-help readers here, thank you

Are you a serial reader of self-help books? If so, enough is enough. Reading self-help books makes you feel good, it gives you a sense that you are 'doing something' toward improving your life. I know, I used to be a serial self-help reader myself! But the upshot is that unless you choose to act on what you read, you are simply playing the 'waiting game', like everyone else. Self-help books are intended to be a catalyst for change. You, and only you, can use that catalyst — the motivation and the tools a book gives you — to effect change. Please don't read this book unless you are seriously committed to actually making changes in your life. If you are not yet at that point — and you will know whether you are or not — please pass this book on to someone else who will actually benefit from reading it (I did warn you — I don't mince my words!). This book is for those who are truly ready to become clear about what they want in life and make it happen.

Be ready to act

As I have already mentioned, it is not enough for me that you simply enjoy reading this book (though clearly as the writer I'd find that highly desirable!). Nor is it sufficient that you simply reflect on its content and complete the exercises. These things alone will not make any tangible difference to your life. Nothing in your life will ever change, until you change the way you act. Change comes from doing things differently, making different choices and behaving in a different way. This book gives you the tools and strategies you need to be able to live a life you love. Are you ready to act differently in order to live a different life?

'If you do what you've always done,
you'll get what you've always got.'

— W.L. Bateman

1

The Waiting Epidemic

What are you waiting for?

'If you are not giving the world the best you have,
what world are you saving it for?'

— Kent Keith

The Waiting Epidemic

How many times have you heard someone say, 'one day I would love to ...', or 'if I ever win lotto I'm going to ...'? Most people have some idea of what they would like to have, or do, 'one day' — or at least know which aspects of their current lives are no longer working for them, and thus, what they would like to change. Start a business, change career, move house, relocate to another city or country, end a relationship that's no longer working, travel, retrain, start a family, write a book, run a marathon ... the possibilities are endless. Yet instead of taking the necessary action to make these things happen ... people wait.

Some people wait until they have finished having a family, or until their children are older or the children have left home. Others wait until they have 'more' — more money, more time or more energy. They wait, oblivious to the fact that the time will never be 'just right'. There will always be another 'something' they need to wait for.

People wait for a future point in time, for the passing of a particular milestone, believing that then, and only then (as if somehow miraculously), they will be able to start living life as they want. In reality however, more often than not, people spend their entire lives 'waiting'. A 'condition' I have termed the 'Waiting Epidemic'.

Those who don't know what they want in life also wait. They wait until they know what they want (and yet seemingly do very little to actually clarify their wants, as though they believe that if they only wait long enough, the answer will magically come to them). Many of these people literally spend their lifetime waiting to know what it is they want.

Think about it. Isn't life too short, too precious, to spend it 'waiting'?

Of course it is. And yet that didn't stop me allowing myself to be a victim of the Waiting Epidemic too. Prior to training as a Life Coach, I worked in various roles in the public sector. While I generally enjoyed my work, it wasn't what I wanted to be doing (although I couldn't articulate what I *did* want). I had a growing sense that something was 'missing'. So what did I do? I stayed where I was. It was easy to stay. The department was a fantastic employer. I enjoyed the company of my colleagues. I knew what was required of me and I was good at my job. The weeks became months. Eighteen months, to be specific. I felt 'stuck'. I didn't know what I wanted to do, or how to even *start* knowing.

Then one day, something inside me changed. I realised, as if in a 'light-bulb moment', that unless I did something to change my situation, nothing was going to change. My perfect job wasn't going to find me — I'd already waited 18 months for that to happen and that approach hadn't worked! I had to find it. My search began in earnest. The process led me to life coaching and, after three years of training, graduating from Coach U, the world's largest coach training organisation.

So you can see that I am highly experienced at waiting, myself. I know that waiting to live the life you want is often the easier, more comfortable path. But I also know, based both on my own experience, and on that of my clients, that we can't live the extraordinary lives we are here to live, until we stop waiting. People comment on how driven and motivated I am. There is nothing special or different about me. It's just that my days of waiting to do the things I want to do are in the past. If you haven't done so already, I hope you will soon choose to make the same choice for yourself.

Life is intended to be lived fully, not limited by our fears, not lived 'safely'. Life is meant to be 'taken by the balls'.

Proactive versus passive living

People tend to live their lives in one of two ways — proactively or passively.

I suggest that the Waiting Epidemic affects about 90 per cent of people. In other words, nine out of every ten people spend their lives 'waiting'. These people are passive in their approach to life. To a greater or lesser extent, they spend much of their time wishing and hoping for things to be different and may complain endlessly about the aspects of their lives that aren't working, as though they have little or no control over them. They buy Lotto tickets in a bid to be happier. They resent others who are successful, and yet do nothing to actively create their own success. They act like victims and have a victim mentality. Passive living is an unfortunate, life-limiting symptom of the Waiting Epidemic.

In contrast, the remaining 10 per cent of people live very differently. They are proactive in their approach to life. They are the people who take their lives in their hands and make things happen. They believe they are capable of achieving great things in life, and so they do. They are clear about what they want for themselves (because they have done the work to know) and take the necessary action to ensure those things come to fruition. These people understand that if they want something in life, it is up to them to make it happen. They realise that creating their own future necessitates continually putting themselves 'out there' in new and different situations. These are the people you read about as having achieved great personal wealth and success. Members of this group know nothing about the

The Passive-living–Proactive-living Continuum

PASSIVE LIVING ⬅

People who live passively:

> 'respond' to life, rather than 'create' it

> take little responsibility for their choices

> complain about their current situation yet do little (if anything) to change it

> resent others' success

> stay within their 'comfort zone'.

Waiting Epidemic — they are too busy creating and living fantastic and fulfilling lives!

Hope is not a strategy for a fulfilling life

It astounds me that so many people choose to live life passively. And yet, it is also completely understandable. Those who live passively convince themselves that 'everything will be okay once ...'. While they tend not to be overly happy with their lot in life in the present day (in fact, some are nothing short of miserable), they manage these feelings of dissatisfaction by maintaining a positive outlook for the future, knowing that 'one day' everything will be 'different', 'better'. This unfailing hope in what the future holds for them allows them to continue to feel okay about themselves in the present.

> Most people go to their graves having lived lives that are nothing like those they could have lived, had they chosen to live proactively rather than passively.

PROACTIVE LIVING

People who live proactively:

> are clear about what they want, and make it happen

> take full responsibility for their choices

> believe in their ability to achieve great things (and so they do)

> applaud and are inspired by others' success

> continually 'put themselves out there'.

But hope is not a strategy. Hope in itself does not make those 'one day' goals a reality. At some point the waiting needs to stop, and the proactive living, the taking action towards one's goals, needs to begin. Sadly, for most, it never does. However unsatisfying life might be, it is also comfortable, familiar and safe.

Valid reasons versus excuses

There will always be situations in which we may legitimately need to wait for something else to occur, before we can do something. Granted. Other times (the majority of times, I suggest), the 'legitimate reasons' are nothing more than 'excuses' for our inaction, which is born out of fear.

For a period of time I told myself that I couldn't possibly give up my well-paid job because I was a solo mother with a son to support. I told myself that 'one day' I would do something I truly felt passionate about, but for now I needed to be 'sensible' and stay where I was. Thank goodness I woke up to the fact that it was my fear talking. Sure, I had to be careful financially, but I hope I would have been irrespective of whether or not I had a child to support. In practice, being 'sensible' meant choosing to build my business to a certain level before resigning from my full-time employment. It didn't mean I couldn't pursue work I loved, it simply influenced how I went about it.

I sincerely believe that if you want something in life there is a way to make it happen. The trouble is, so often people put their energy into focusing on potential obstacles or creating excuses, rather than finding solutions and just getting on with making it happen.

Let's look at some commonly used excuses. I wonder if you can identify with any of them?

Scenario	John no longer enjoys his job (in fact he hasn't for some time).
Excuse for passive inaction	'The job market's so quiet at the moment, I wouldn't find anything else and even if I did, it wouldn't pay enough. It's just not the right time to be looking for new work. Besides, I don't even have a current CV.'
Proactive response	'I have just updated my CV, and have appointments with three recruitment companies next week.'

Scenario	Vanessa is overweight and has been advised by her doctor to lose 15 kg.
Excuse for passive inaction	'I work long hours and just don't have the time to exercise. Sure, I know I could eat healthier, but by the time I get home from work, cooking is the last thing I want to do. It will be easier once this project is finished.'
Proactive response	'I have started setting my alarm to go off 30 minutes earlier and using the time to go for a brisk walk each morning before work. I also found this fantastic website which has heaps of easy-to-prepare, healthy recipes. I am feeling much better already.'

Scenario	Sarah has always wanted to set up her own graphic design business.
Excuse for passive inaction	'I don't have enough time at present. Even though the kids are at school now, I still need to be available for them after school. What if they're sick, and what am I supposed to do during the school holidays? It's just not that easy.'
Proactive response	'I have just finished writing a business plan. I will work from home, and initially only three days a week, from 9 a.m. to 3 p.m. This way I won't miss out on time with my kids, yet get to finally do what I've always wanted to. I am so excited.'

Scenario	Jenny was an avid horse-rider in her teens. Now a mother of two teenagers herself, she is always talking about riding again.
Excuse for passive inaction	'I wouldn't even know how to get started. Besides, riding's not cheap and we're financially stretched as it is. And it's been so long, I don't even know if I could still get on a horse! One day …'
Proactive response	'I found out about a local equestrian centre online and am now riding twice a week. It's not costing anything like as much as I thought it would. I love it. I wish I'd gone back to it years ago.'

Scenario	Jacob is a keen runner, and has frequently toyed with the idea of running a marathon.
Excuse for passive inaction	'Training for a marathon is a big commitment. It wouldn't be fair on my family. And given I travel a bit with work, it would just be too hard to fit the training in.'
Proactive response	'I've registered for my first marathon and am well on track with my training. My family is incredibly supportive. Sometimes the kids even bike along beside me when I'm training. It's great.'

It is often much easier to identify passive living in others than it is to recognise the same symptoms in ourselves (initially, at least). Chances are that you are surrounded by people who talk about what they will do 'one day' yet never seem to make it happen. I encourage you to listen carefully to those around you. What is it they talk of wanting? What excuses do they give? And what about yourself? To what extent are you also afflicted by the Waiting Epidemic? What are your equivalent examples to those given above?

THE WAITING EPIDEMIC

What are you currently waiting for? Why?

How would you complete the following sentence? (You may have several answers.)

'One day, once/when .... , I would love to ....'

To what extent are you living or just existing?

Where are you currently on the Passive-living–Proactive-living continuum? To what extent are you 'letting life happen to you' or 'making life happen'?

Where would you like to be on the Passive-living–Proactive-living continuum?

What is really stopping you from living more proactively?

The truth about fear

What is really stopping you?

'Life begins at the end of your comfort zone.'

— Neale Donald Walsch

'Feel the fear and do it anyway.'

— Susan Jeffers

The Waiting Epidemic and fear

What is behind this Waiting Epidemic? Why are so many people seemingly happy with living so passively?

The answer is simple: fear.

The Waiting Epidemic exists because people allow fear to stop them taking action towards achieving what they want in life. People 'wait to live' because they are scared to 'put themselves out there'.

Change the way you think about fear

Most people react somewhat negatively (initially at least) to the notion that it is fear that is stopping them from achieving what they want in life. 'I'm not afraid … it's just that I can't … until …' — and out rolls the list of other things that need to happen first. We don't like to admit that we are afraid. We see it as a weakness. Instead, we subconsciously create valid reasons why we can't do something, or at least why we can't do it *right now*. Rather than face our fears and act despite them, we take the path of least resistance and allow them to stop us from taking action. Or worse, we retreat.

If you are serious about making your goals happen, you need to change the way you think about fear.

The fact is, it's impossible to live life fully if you continue to let fear stop you taking action.

Let's begin by clarifying what fear is.

Understanding fear

Everyone experiences fear – fear is 'normal'

It's funny how we often assume that we are the only ones who feel or experience life in the way we do. It's as though we think we are programmed to react to situations in a way that is different from everyone else. When it comes to fear, we are not unique.

Everyone, without exception, experiences fear when trying something new. Fear is normal.

As young children, we are programmed to be careful, to be risk averse and to put safety first. How often, when you were a child, did your parents tell you to 'be careful' or to 'take care', as opposed to 'go and do something scary today' or 'go and take a risk'? Research tells us that the average child is exposed 160,000 times to messages of 'no, you can't' by the age of 18. This is significantly more than the 10,000 times a child hears 'yes, you can' during the same period. The messages we grow up with are disproportionately negative. 'Be careful' suggests that the world is a scary and dangerous place. 'No, you can't' reinforces that there are limits to what one can or should do.

Together, such messages have a significant impact on how most people go on to lead their lives as adults. People are comfortable with what is familiar to them. They feel 'safe'. They are familiar with their environment, they have established ways of behaving, of doing the things they usually do, and of interacting with others — whom they know well. They feel 'okay' in the world. And mostly, in control. This is often referred to as a person's comfort zone.

Comfort zones definitely have their benefits in that they allow us to feel safe by keeping us in familiar territory. However, they are not so advantageous when it comes to wanting to achieve more in life. In fact, they work against us. As soon as you start taking action toward a new goal, putting yourself in a new situation and trying something you are unfamiliar with, you automatically step outside your comfort zone. And consequently you feel uncomfortable. Sometimes, *very* uncomfortable. It is at this point that too many people react to this often unexpected emotion, and stop. Some interpret their fear as a sign to retreat, or choose to wait until they feel more comfortable. They wait for the fear to subside, yet it never will, and years pass in the meantime (hence we have a Waiting Epidemic).

If you want to change things in your life, for the better, you need to become comfortable with being uncomfortable.

It is impossible to stretch yourself to have and be more, without stepping outside your comfort zone.

Choose to act despite fear

The trick here is to choose to feel excited when you feel uncomfortable or anxious. Experiencing fear means you are outside your comfort zone and on your way to creating or doing something new. It means you are moving closer to achieving your goal — or goals. Even the world's most successful people experience fear, doubt and worry. Everyone does. The difference is that these people have already learnt what you are learning now — that being uncomfortable, feeling fear, is normal.

Fear is a natural part of being on the path to success.

In the previous chapter I distinguished between those who live passively and those who live proactively. Those who live passively stay within their comfort zones. They choose to stay with the status quo, rather than risk feeling scared or uncomfortable. Those who live proactively, on the other hand, choose to step outside their comfort zones and to take action, despite feeling uncomfortable. They don't let fear stop them. Again, the key difference between these two groups has nothing to do with *feeling* fear — both groups feel fear. The difference lies in whether they *allow* fear to stop them pursuing their dreams.

> *'True courage is not the absence of fear,*
> *it's in the mastery of fear.'*
>
> — Mark Twain

Successful people consistently try new things. I am sure you can think of examples from your own life when you have been in a new situation, perhaps starting a new job, or attending a function or event where you knew few people, when your anxiety levels were initially high. Learning to drive is a good example. When most people begin learning to drive a car, they are anxious. They feel nervous. The 'what if I don't pass my driver's test?' voice starts in their head. 'I keep stalling the car. What if I never get this right?' I have met people who have chosen to spend their lives unable to drive, rather than risk feeling uncomfortable, and putting themselves 'out there'. And yet the majority of people — and probably you included — have been sufficiently motivated by the desire for independence that, despite feeling the fear, they have successfully learnt how to drive. Staying with this example, what happened to your fear and anxiety as you became a more experienced driver? The fear disappeared. You stretched yourself, you felt uncomfortable but didn't let this stop you. You learned to drive, and as you acquired this new skill, it became part of what is familiar to you, part of your (new) 'comfort zone' and the fear dissipated accordingly.

And so it is with fear. Fear will accompany any new task (that's a given), but ONLY UNTIL you become confident and master that task, then the fear will disappear.

> *'Do the things you fear*
> *and the fear will disappear.'*
>
> — David Joseph Schwartz

Best of all, it will disappear leaving you with your goal achieved AND feeling 10 feet tall and bullet-proof! Acting, despite fear, makes you feel great. It's like a reward for having the courage to put yourself out there.

Let me share with you some of the fantastic choices my clients have made for themselves. Matthew, once a sought-after cardiac specialist, is now pursuing his passion for food, successfully running his own fine-dining restaurant.

Pam, a grandmother, left her loveless marriage after 32 years and has just completed a degree in counselling. Emma, a stay-at-home mother of three, now has her own clothing design label and recently secured a huge contract with one of Australia's leading retail chains. Joshua and his wife Mandy left their respective teaching jobs and are currently in South East Asia, somewhere they have always wanted to explore (did I mention they're in their fifties?).

The common theme to these stories is that they all involve people consciously choosing to step outside their comfort zones to finally live the lives they'd been waiting (for quite some time in some cases) to live. Do you think they felt scared, unsure or had any doubts? You bet! Did they act on their dreams and goals despite that fear? Yes. Putting yourself out there into previously uncharted ground (for you) isn't easy, but it is absolutely worth it. I know Matthew, Pam, Emma, Joshua and Mandy certainly agree.

Let the fear of staying 'stuck' motivate you

If you are struggling with the notion of acting despite fear, let's consider this from a different angle for a moment.

Fear, as we have discussed, often keeps people from taking the actions required to move them from where they are now, to where they want to be. They feel 'stuck', almost paralysed by fear. Putting themselves out there, stepping out of their comfort zone, simply feels too hard.

When working with a client who is letting fear stop them, I will often question how well their current strategy of not taking action is working for them. I encourage you to consider this same question: 'Is your current strategy of letting fear stop you from achieving all that you could in life, working for you?'

If you allow yourself to be or to stay stuck, unable to take action toward creating a better life for yourself because

Allowing fear (the fear of failing or of what others might think of you) to stop you going after your goals is to accept the status quo as 'your lot'.

What scares you the most – the thought of 'putting yourself out there' or the thought of spending the rest of your life as you are at present?

you feel uncomfortable or scared, you are in effect accepting your current life as 'enough' for you. While you might talk of wanting things to change, until you actually allow yourself to take action, nothing will change. Be honest with yourself about whether your decisions are truly reflective of what you want most in life.

Instead of allowing fear to stop you, allow the greater fear of never achieving what you could be (or have) in life, motivate you.

This certainly works for me. Whenever I catch myself 'stalling' — feeling anxious prior to speaking to a particularly large group, or nervous just before taking the floor at a major dancesport competition — I remind myself that I am not here to live a small life (or at least smaller than is possible). I am here to live big; to live a full and extraordinary life. And frankly, the thought of living small, of never getting my message out to the world or never daring to compete at the highest level of competition, scares me more than anything else. Given the choice of feeling comfortable and living small, or feeling uncomfortable and scared at times and living an extraordinary life, I say 'bring on the discomfort and fear!'

'I'd rather attempt to do something great and fail than to attempt to do nothing and succeed.'

— Robert H. Schuller

Reflective questions

THE TRUTH ABOUT FEAR

What would you do differently if you knew that you could not fail?

What, specifically, are you most afraid of?
(Is it fear of 'failing', of what others might think, of succeeding ... ?)

Are you willing to accept the status quo as your lot in life? How does the thought of that make you feel?

For you personally, what is worse, the thought of failing to achieve your goals, or of never even trying?

What decision do you need to make?

Take responsibilty for your life

What are you currently choosing for yourself?

'If it's to be, it's up to me.'

— William Johnsen

Taking responsibility for your own life is a prerequisite to being able to achieve your goals and dreams.

Yet, despite most people being quick to claim they take responsibility, few actually do.

Understanding responsibility

It is easy to take responsibility for our actions, when things go well. We happily take the credit when we have successfully closed a deal at work, or when someone compliments us on a job well done. We feel good about ourselves. We internalise our successes and attribute them to internally controlled factors, such as skill and effort.

In contrast, we tend to be far less prepared to take responsibility for our actions when things go less well. If we miss a deadline at work, we can be quick to find an excuse, or someone or something, to blame. 'There was no way I could get the report done on time, the information I needed just wasn't available', or 'I would have closed the deal if I'd just had a bit more time'.

> Taking responsibility for your life involves fully accepting that you, and only you, are responsible for the choices you make and what happens as a consequence of those choices.

Likewise in non-work situations. 'How am I supposed to lose weight when my husband keeps bringing home chocolate? He knows I shouldn't be eating it.' We tend to externalise failure and attribute it to externally controlled factors, such as other people or circumstances, things we cannot personally control. By doing so, by not taking full personal responsibility for our failures, we keep our self-esteem intact. We can continue to feel okay about ourselves, despite disappointing outcomes.

Why taking responsibility matters

Being responsible for something means being able to be held to account for it. Taking full responsibility for oneself is an incredibly liberating, powerful place to reach. While it means accepting (being honest about) your shortcomings, and owning your failures as well as your successes, it also means realising that you are in full control of your life and the choices you make. It is this vital realisation that will enable you to climb into the driver's seat of your life.

> As soon as you take full responsibility for your life – you are in charge. There ceases to be limits on what you, as an individual, can do, be or have. Powerful stuff!

'Accept responsibility for your life.
Know that it is you who will get you
where you want to go, no one else.'

— Les Brown

Four key aspects of taking responsibility for your life

If you are truly taking responsibility for yourself you will:

> ❭ stop blaming others (as you, and only you, are responsible)

> ❭ stop complaining (now that you own your feelings, there's no longer a need to justify them to others)

> ❭ stop making excuses (as you no longer need to make excuses)

> ❭ stop caring what others think (now that you are happily responsible for the choices you make).

Let's take a moment to explore each of these.

1. Stop blaming others

How often do you hear people complain about their situations, or about something someone else has done to them? 'I can't believe she did that ...' or 'How am I supposed to be happy when he keeps ...'. Some people spend their entire lives moaning and complaining about unhappy experiences in their past and blaming their problems or current circumstances on other people. It is easy to unknowingly fall into the trap of holding other people responsible for what happens in our life and how we consequently feel. On some level it makes us feel better about ourselves.

Parents are the most popular targets. Even as adults, most people feel some degree of anger toward one or both parents, for something they did — or did not — do during one's childhood.

'Parents can only give good advice or put them on the right paths, but the final forming of a person's character lies in their own hands.'

— Anne Frank

Think about someone in your life with whom you are angry. It may be your spouse, a friend, or a parent. Be clear about why you are angry — what have they done? How do your feelings around this 'fit' with the idea that, ultimately, you and only you, are responsible for how you feel and behave? What shift do you need to make (you, not the other person) if you are to truly start taking responsibility for your own life? How will this shift change how you feel in relation to the other person?

When you take responsibility for your own thoughts, actions and emotions, you no longer need to blame others. You stop giving your power away. You realise that you, and you alone, are fully responsible for what is in your life (the good and also the not-so-good).

2. Stop complaining

'You are where you are today because you have chosen to be there.'

— Harry Browne

Think about it. You are where you are today, because of the decisions you have made in your life up until now. Not as a

Much of our complaining is us justifying our negative emotions – 'I am only this upset because she didn't even have the courtesy to ...' or 'I can't believe he would do this to me ...'. But if you are in control of your life, including how you choose to react and respond to the actions of others, then what's there to complain about?

consequence of what happened to you when you were a child, or what your parents did or did not do, but because of the decisions you have made and the ways you have chosen to react or respond to the consequences of these decisions.

Don't allow 'her' to upset you. Stop letting 'him' frustrate you. Taking responsibility for your life includes taking responsibility for your emotions. Eleanor Roosevelt's famous quote, 'No one can make you feel inferior without your consent,' reinforces this too. No one can 'make you feel' a certain way. Only you can. As soon as you start taking full responsibility for your life, you will find you have nothing left to complain about.

Imagine a complaint-free you. How different would that be? How much 'lighter' would you feel?

I encourage you to listen to yourself very carefully from now on. If you hear yourself complaining about anything at all, stop, and reflect on what's going on — what are you not taking responsibility for here? Rather than complaining, use that same energy to identify a thought pattern that is more appropriate for someone who is now taking full responsibility. Become a complaint-free zone. Notice the shift in how you feel. Enjoy the lightness.

3. Stop making excuses

'People spend too much energy finding excuses for not being what they are capable of being, and not enough energy putting themselves on the line, growing out of the past, and getting on with their lives.'

— J. Michael Straczynski

Making excuses is common practice. Why? For most people, making excuses is a habit; an automatic, self-protective mechanism that enables them to continue to feel good about themselves, when things don't go their way in life. Excuses provide us with an 'out': typically an externally based nothing-to-do-with-us reason for non-performance. Excuses allow us to rationalise what might otherwise be seen as a failure, and keep us feeling good about ourselves. In so doing, they keep us from having to own or take responsibility for our shortcomings. However, they also keep us 'living small'.

When you start taking full responsibility for your life, you will no longer make excuses. You will step up and own your actions when things don't go your way. You will no longer require reasons or justifications to explain why you can't go after whatever you want in life. You won't need to: you will be out there doing it!

Start tuning in to the people around you and notice when and where people are making excuses. You will soon realise how prevalent this practice is. Become aware of your own behaviour too. When things don't quite go your way, listen to your internal voice. Choose to become an 'excuse-free zone'. Consider the following:

> What excuses do you typically use?

> What excuses are you hiding behind right now?

> What is really stopping you from having, being or doing all that you could?

> What is a more appropriate response for someone who is now taking full responsibility for their life?

4. Stop caring what others think

Worrying about what others think can be a real hindrance. 'What will they think if I ... ?' or 'Can you imagine what she'd say if I ... ?'

People are often so much more concerned about what others will think of them if they do (or don't do) something, than what they think of themselves.

It's as though people's own wants or desires become secondary to those of everyone else. At the end of the day, whose life is this?

It's not always easy to ignore the opinions of others, but it is a skill that, like any, gets easier the more we do it. Sure, you may still be aware of others' views, but the key is to stop letting those views influence your decisions about your own life. After all, you and only you — no one else — can be responsible for your life.

The next time you have a decision to make, be aware of the extent to which you are letting other people's views impact on your decision making. Does it really matter what others think? Are you allowing their view to be more important to you than your own? Awareness of someone else's perspective is one thing, but ultimately — given that you alone are responsible for the choices you make — allow yourself the privilege of making decisions based only on what you personally think and feel is right for you. Notice how empowering this is.

'It is not what happens to you but how you respond to what happens that determines whether you are happy or unhappy.'

— Brian Tracy

TAKE RESPONSIBILITY FOR YOUR LIFE

To what extent do you believe you have the power to create your own future through the choices you make?

To what extent are you taking full responsibility for your life?

In what areas could you accept more personal responsibility? What's the first step?

What would you do if you knew that no one would judge you? What else?

What gift are you not being responsible for? What are you avoiding?

Know you can
handle anything

*'You can handle anything
if you think you can.'*

— Smiley Blanton

How different would your life be if you absolutely, whole-heartedly *knew* that you could handle anything that came your way? Think about it.

The power of your inner voice

We have already discussed the extent to which people allow their fears to keep them from achieving what they are capable of.

People feel anxious when they put themselves out there, in new situations. It's a natural response to the unfamiliar. 'Will I be able to do this?' 'What if I don't know anyone?' 'What if I make a fool of myself?' Our internal chatterbox is far too efficient at filling our heads with messages of self-doubt. No wonder we feel anxious and scared! How different our experience would be if, instead of hearing these negative messages, we were able to reprogramme our chatterbox to be positive! 'No matter what happens, I can handle this.' Wow, what a difference. A life-changing difference!

Reprogramme your fear-based negative inner voice to be an action-inspiring 'I-can-handle-anything' voice.

Putting ourselves in unfamiliar territory and trying new things will always cause us to feel some level of anxiety or fear. No matter who you are, what you do, or how successful you become, that will never change. That is not the part we can control or change. Our focus here is on our response to those feelings of fear — the area in which we *can* change things for the better.

Recognise your own strength

I encourage you to think back to some of the obstacles you have faced in your life. Think of the most difficult, challenging times you've experienced. You handled those situations or events. They may have been hard. They may have taken considerable time to recover from, but the fact is that you handled what came your way. It is what we do. And we carry on, often giving ourselves little credit for how strong and resilient we are. Think about your past. You have handled everything that has come your way. Recognise your own strength.

I was twelve years old when my father committed suicide. According to UN data, up to 36 percent of girls and 29 per cent of boys worldwide have been sexually abused as children. The WHO reports that cancer accounts for one in every eight deaths globally. I could go on.

My point is that 'stuff' happens in life: some we celebrate, some we would never wish for. What do we do? We handle it. Every time. Without exception. We — and this includes you — can handle anything.

Recognise your own strength and allow this to empower you to achieve what you want in life.

'To believe in yourself is the greatest step
you can take to succeed.'

— Author unknown

Realising you can handle anything is what will enable you to act, despite your fear.

Acknowledging your own strength in this way is an important step in changing the way you think about fear (as is shown in the diagram below). It makes sense. Why would you choose to act, despite fear, if you doubted your ability to handle what might happen? You wouldn't act. And thus, most people

Achieving your goals despite your fear

Acknowledge that you feel anxious/fearful about putting yourself out there.

Understand that fear is normal, that everyone experiences fear in new situations.

Know that you can handle anything.

Act despite your fear. Make it happen.

Feel fantastic about yourself.

Be successful in achieving your goal (or moving closer to achieving your goal).

Once you've achieved your first goal, feel motivated, inspired and excited to achieve an even bigger goal.

don't. You can see how important it is to trust yourself to handle anything that comes your way. It is critical.

The 'I can handle anything' affirmation

You may or may not be a great user of affirmations. I wasn't until I learnt the power of this one sentence, 'I can handle anything'.

I don't have screeds of positive affirmations written on small pieces of paper dotted throughout my house. That works well for some people, but it's not for me. There is just one affirming phrase that I use. It is with me constantly in my head. I recall it regularly throughout each and every day. It empowers me in an instant every time I say it to myself.

'I can handle anything.'

I encourage you to try it.

Begin by writing it down where you will see it. Do whatever you need to do to see it frequently throughout your day. You are reprogramming your brain. The more you expose yourself to positive, self-affirming messages, the more easily you will be able to discount or counter any negative 'but what if I fail?', 'what if I can't do this?' or 'what if other people think I'm stupid?' fear-based thoughts. We want to turn up the volume on positive messages to such an extent that you can no longer hear the negative, self-limiting voices within you. Those voices will always be there. Chances are they have been with you throughout your childhood. They are well-established, deep-rooted thought patterns. And they are stubborn, but not so stubborn that we can't change them.

Choose to listen to a new 'station'

Using the analogy of different radio stations, it is important for you to recognise that you actually have a choice of

Choose to stop listening to your negative inner self – 'switch stations' and tune into a more positive, life-enhancing 'I can handle anything' inner voice.

what 'station' (inner voice messages) you choose to listen to. Up until now, you have probably tuned into your negative voice (our default station from birth). However, there is an alternative and I encourage you to 'switch stations', as it were. Rather than continuing to tune into your negative voice, choose to 'upgrade' to a more positive, life-enhancing, feel-good alternative — the 'I can handle anything' station.

Reflective questions

KNOW YOU CAN HANDLE ANYTHING

What have been your greatest challenges or the most difficult times in your life? Acknowledge and give yourself credit for handling these. What did these experiences show you about your inner strength and your ability to handle anything?

What will it take for you to 'switch stations' and tune into the 'I can handle anything' station? And what will you do to ensure that you stay tuned in to this more positive, self-affirming station from now on?

Choose to live a 'kick-arse life'

'It is not the length of life, but the depth of it.'

— Ralph Waldo Emerson

'Everything was impossible until somebody did it.'

— Scott Dinsmore

To me, the term 'kick-arse life' comes close to encapsulating the approach that I advocate.

Live a 'kick-arse life'	=	Be clear about what you want, make it big, make it matter and make it happen.

I encourage you to keep repeating this phrase, 'be clear about what you want, make it big, make it matter and make it happen' to yourself, until you have memorised it. Have it as your mantra.

It is about living your life fully, consciously and in the present. It is as proactive as the Waiting Epidemic is passive.

Why is it important to be clear about what you want, make it big, make it matter and make it happen?

The answer is simple: it will make you happier.

> *'The greatest need of human beings is for*
> *a sense of meaning and purpose in life,*
> *for a goal to work toward.'*

— Viktor Frankl

When people work toward and achieve a goal that truly matters to them, they feel energised, focused, and excited about life.

As humans we naturally seek a sense of purpose and/or accomplishment in areas that are important and meaningful to us. We like to contribute, to feel a part of something bigger than ourselves, to make a difference, to feel as though our lives have meaning. It makes us feel good. It gives sense to our being here.

To better understand why they are so important, let's take a closer look at each of the four aspects of living a kick-arse life:

1. Be clear about what you want in life.

2. Make it big.

3. Make it matter.

4. Make it happen.

1. Be clear about what you want in life

As I have already said, many times, the whole point of being alive is — surely — to live, and to live fully and consciously.

'May you live all of the days of your life.'

— Jonathan Swift

Knowing what you want — what you really, really want — in life, is a fundamental requisite to living fully. Deciding what you want in life paves the way for living your best life. It puts *you* in control of your future.

'If you don't know what you want then you will end up working for or following someone who does. Anytime you are not hard at work on your own agenda, you are working for somebody else's.'

— Andrew Halfacre

When I first came across this quote I had to read it a couple of times to fully comprehend the strength of the truth it speaks. You may choose to reread it yourself. Surely life is too precious, too short to spend it in anything but a leading role. This is your life. Choose to spend it centre-stage — not standing left-of-stage being told what costume to wear by someone else sitting in the director's chair. Deciding what you want is the way to write the script of your very own screenplay.

The following chapters provide a framework for you to know what you want in life. It is a process that works.

2. Make it big

When it comes to truly living your life, size *does* matter!

'Think big, believe big, act big and the results will be big.'

— Anonymous

As you begin to consider what you want for yourself, decide now, to make 'it' big (whatever 'it' is). Achieving a great goal requires persistence, inner strength, and unfailing motivation. I summarise these as 'passion'. It is difficult to maintain such a level of desire, if what you want is relatively small or ordinary. You need your desire to be strong, all-consuming even, so that your eagerness for your goal will be such that it will keep you on track even when you get weary along the way.

> *'Desire is the starting point of all achievement, not a hope, not a wish, but a keen pulsating desire which transcends everything.'*

— Napoleon Hill

How big is 'big'?

'How big is big?' you ask. Big enough that the thought of it makes you feel both excited and scared at the same time. Nervous, yet intrigued. A 'big' goal is one that will stretch you. That is, one that will require you to step outside your comfort zone and into unfamiliar territory. It will make you feel uncomfortable. It is supposed to!

Of course, what is a big goal for one person may not seem so big for another. It will depend on your starting point. For example, setting a goal of running five kilometres three times a week may initially feel like a big goal for a non-runner, whereas for a more experienced runner, setting a goal of running a half or full marathon might be the equivalent big goal.

Big goals, by nature of their ability to stretch you, are — as we have already discussed — very powerful. Take the example above, again. Which option is more exciting or inspiring: running five kilometres or running a marathon?

And taking a different example, which is more exciting or inspiring: looking for a new job doing what you currently do, only elsewhere, or finally starting that business you have always wanted to in a completely different industry?

It is almost as though big goals have a magnetic force that draws you toward them.

Big goals excite you, inspire you, scare you and make you feel alive – the vital ingredients that will not only get you in action, but keep you in action.

> *'Dream big dreams; only big dreams have the power to move men's souls.'*
>
> — Marcus Aurelius

Continuously stretch yourself

I advocate actively working toward at least one huge, gigantic, fantastic goal that stretches you (and seriously puts you outside your comfort zone), at any one time. Choose a goal that, once accomplished, will have the most significantly positive impact on your life.

> *'Do what you think you cannot do.'*
>
> — Eleanor Roosevelt

This will ensure you are never standing still, always challenging yourself, always feeling inspired and excited, always putting yourself out there beyond your comfort zone, and always moving forward.

Of course, not all of the things you will identify as wanting will necessarily be big or require significant change. They won't. But allowing yourself to think big may enable you to see possibilities and identify ideas you would not otherwise consider. Often it only takes one gem of an idea to change the direction of your life. Be open to finding your own gem as you complete the exercises in this book.

3. Make it matter

It makes sense that what you choose for yourself in life needs to matter deeply to you. We have already talked about the fact that working toward and achieving a goal fulfils our sense of purpose and makes us feel good. For this sense of purpose and/or accomplishment to 'sustain us' (allow us to continue to feel good over the medium to longer term), what we are doing also needs to be important and meaningful to us.

Statistics suggest that up to 80 per cent of people are doing work they don't enjoy. Put another way, four out of every five people spend a third of their lives doing something that makes them unhappy. Isn't that alarming! I suggest this figure is so high simply because people aren't doing work that matters to them. Few people — too few, clearly — give any consideration to what personally matters most to them when job-hunting or choosing their careers. People tend to look for work that is a good fit for their skills and experience, that preferably pays well, and that, if they are lucky, is something they will enjoy. I suggest that few people consider what most matters to them. Yet the upshot is that if what you are doing and how you choose to spend your time doesn't matter sufficiently to you, you won't enjoy it. You may initially, but not over the longer term.

Does the work you are currently doing truly matter to you? Does the way you choose to spend your time reflect what personally matters most to you?

There was certainly a point in my life in which my responses to both of these questions would have been a resounding 'no'. I 'kind of' enjoyed my work, but knew it wasn't me. I wanted to make a positive, meaningful difference in people's lives. I wanted to make my dent on the world. I kept hearing how 'important' my work was. And yes, within the context of the government department

I worked for, the reports I wrote and the advice I gave to Ministers did matter. But not to me — at least not in a deeply personal way. That's the bit that was missing. That's the bit I suggest is missing for far too many people.

I am now doing work that does truly matter to me. And the difference in how I feel when I get out of bed each morning is extraordinary.

As you begin to consider what it is that you want for yourself (not only in relation to work, but in every area of your life), I encourage you to keep focused on what matters most to you. Knowing your personal values (covered later in this book) will help you with this. Let what really matters to you be a key input into the decisions you're about to make.

4. Make it happen

Of the four aspects of living a kick-arse life — be clear about what you want, make it big, make it matter and make it happen — making it happen is unquestionably the point at which your life changes.

You could be clear about what you want in life, make it big and make it matter (the first three elements), but until you make it happen, nothing in your life will change. Making it happen requires action. And now. Making it happen means you stop waiting, stop making excuses, and stop letting fear stop you. It requires you to step into the driver's seat and start living big, exciting, life-changing goals.

> If everyone chose to live a kick-arse life, the worldwide phenomenon of waiting would cease. The Waiting Epidemic would be over.

So I think it's clear: making it happen is the ultimate antidote to the Waiting Epidemic!

If you haven't already done so, I challenge you to make the decision right now: decide to stop waiting, and start living your life, effective immediately. It is time to live a kick-arse life. That is, to be clear about what you want, make it big, make it matter and make it happen.

*'Stop wearing your wishbone where
your backbone ought to be.'*

— Elizabeth Gilbert

Reflective questions

CHOOSE TO LIVE A 'KICK-ARSE LIFE'

Are you truly ready to live a 'kick-arse life'? How do you know?

How does the thought of being clear about what you want, making it big, making it matter and making it happen, make you feel?

What is the biggest, most scary goal you can think of? How would this change your life? How do you expect you would feel once you achieved it?

What action can you take today? What is your first/ next step toward living a 'kick-arse life'?

The secret to knowing what you want in life

'There are no great people in this world, only great challenges which ordinary people rise to meet.'

— William Frederick Halsey Jr.

Are you ready to know the secret to knowing what you want?

> The 'secret' to knowing what you want in life, is this:
>
> **In order to know what you want in life, you must decide what you want in life.**

To know what you want requires a process of reflection and analysis, and ultimately, decision making. It is up to each of us to consciously decide what it is that we want.

I hope that hasn't disappointed you. I'm sorry if you were hoping for or expecting something a little more profound. The truth is that there is no magic wand or crystal ball to enable you to know what you want. Life doesn't work like that.

'The golden opportunity you are seeking is in yourself.'

— Orison Swett Marden

What you need in order to be able to decide what you want

I believe everybody is capable of knowing what it is that they want, as long as they have the following:

1. The right attitude.

2. A framework for clarifying what they want — a process to follow or at least an understanding of the sort of information that is useful to consider.

3. A willingness to do the work required (to know).

4. An understanding of the basics of good decision making.

These four factors are responsible for the fact that so few people know what it is they truly want in their lives. Sometimes people have an unhelpful attitude that hinders their knowing what they want; or they have no idea how to clarify what they want; or they expect they should just know what it is that they want and therefore don't expect, or are not prepared, to do the work required; or they simply don't know how to make decisions.

Let's take a closer look at each of these.

1. The right attitude

Attitude matters. It matters particularly when completing exercises like those in this book that are designed to assist you tap into the answers I know are within you. In order for the exercises to work for you, you need to be fully open to what comes to you. You need to be solution-focused and receptive to the ideas and insights you will uncover. If you are not, they simply will not work.

> *'If you think you can,*
> *or you think you can't*
> *– you are right.'*
>
> — Henry Ford

This isn't a task that can be done half-heartedly. The extent to which you allow these exercises to assist you clarify what you want in life, will determine the extent to which they are effective for you. Check in with yourself right now to gauge how truly ready you are to clarify what you want.

'Well I'll certainly give it my best shot,' you might say, 'I'll try.' I am always concerned when I hear the words 'I'll try'. What does 'trying' actually mean? To me, it's a bit like being told, 'I'll give it a go, but we both know I may not be able to do it.' And of course, approach any new task or exercise with an 'I may not be able to do it' attitude and *voilà*, even before you've started, you have significantly reduced your chance of success — and given yourself a tidy 'out', in case you need it.

> *'Do or do not.*
> *There is no try.'*
>
> — Yoda

Picture this. Sonia is at home, about to put the kids into bed. She suddenly realises she forgot to get some more milk when she was out earlier. She knows there's not enough for breakfast. Aware her husband Jeremy may not have left work yet, she quickly gives him a call. 'Sorry love, do you mind picking up a two-litre bottle of milk on your way home please?' 'Sure, no worries, I'll try to remember,' Jeremy responds. Mmm ... 'try to remember'. It's hardly a guarantee that Jeremy will get the milk, is it? See how the word 'try' gives Jeremy an 'out clause'. If he comes home without the milk, it was just that he didn't remember — but of course, Sonia can't be too harsh on him because he did try, which, after all, is all that he committed to do.

What happens when we remove the word 'try'? Jeremy's reply might become something along the lines of, 'Sure, no worries, I'll get it. See you when I get home'. No longer is he suggesting he will 'try to remember'. He will simply get it. He has made a commitment and is significantly more likely to deliver on it. You can almost feel the difference.

I am raising this here because I do not want you to try to clarify what you want in your life. Please don't try. Either do it, or don't do it. To try is to give yourself an out before you have even begun the exercises. If you choose to continue reading this book, do so as someone who is about to clarify what they want — no ifs or buts. If you are prepared to merely 'try' — take my word for it, your time will almost certainly be better spent going to get that bottle of milk Sonia needs!

'How committed are you?
There is a remarkable difference between
a commitment of 99% and 100%.'

— Vic Conant

2. Knowing HOW to clarify what you want

How do you clarify what you want in life? What do you need to think about? How do you know if you're on the right track? Where do you even start?

Some people grow up very clear about what it is they want for themselves. However, most do not. I believe that the majority of people have little or no idea, what it is that they actually want for themselves. Not because they don't want to know, but because they don't know how to know. And so instead of proactively seeking help to clarify what they want in life, they wait. They wait until they do know. It's as though they believe that if they only wait long enough, 'the answer' will somehow magically come to them.

Much of the remainder of this book is dedicated to helping you identify what you want in life. In the next chapter, I share with you the five-step process that hundreds of my clients have successfully used to identify what they want.

The following chapters take you through the various steps of this process, giving you a host of useful tools and exercises. You will be shown how to know yourself better, identify your values, discover your passions, and ask yourself the right questions, which, when pulled together, give you a strong foundation for deciding what you want — the final step in the process.

3. Willingness to do the work required (to know)

Being clear about what you want and making decisions about your future require time and effort (as do most things in life that are worth doing or having). As I keep saying, unfortunately there is no crystal ball or magic wand. If you are serious about wanting to clarify what you want in life, you must do the work to know. Having a clear process to follow is only as helpful as the extent to which you are prepared to put in the effort to follow or complete that process.

4. Understanding the basics of good decision making

We have already talked about the secret to knowing what you want in life — the fact that knowing what you want requires you to make decisions.

This can be hard. We know also how paralysing fear can be. Too often fear stops people, not only from having what they want in life, but often even from clarifying what they want for themselves.

You need to turn the volume down on those voices that say, 'but what if I get it wrong?', 'but how can I be sure about what I want?' and 'but I just don't know'. Listening to these will only keep you 'stuck' and prevent you from being able to make the decisions that are out there waiting for you to make.

'Yes, but what if I really just don't know what I want?' I hear you say. My response: it's time to raise your standards. It's time to stop being okay with not knowing what you want. Opting not to make any decision, for whatever reason, is in itself a decision, albeit it a passive one. If you want something in life to be different, you need to make different decisions.

Deciding what you want for yourself doesn't have to be as scary or as hard as it may feel right now. As with anything in life, it's how you think about it that influences how you feel about or perceive a certain task. Consider the truths about decision making on the next page.

I hope these will go some way towards helping you feel more comfortable and less fearful about the task ahead of you. You may benefit from coming back and reminding yourself of these points periodically. Let's take a closer look at them.

Truths about decision making

> You, and only you, can know what is right for you.

> You can only ever make the best choice you can, at any given point in time.

> Whatever the outcome, you will handle it.

You, and only you, can know what is right for you

One of the key premises on which coaching is based is that you, and only you, can know what is right for you. As a coach, I help people move from where they are now, to where they want to be. I do not give advice or tell people what I think they should do. Instead, I ask the right questions and share tools and strategies that enable clients to access the information within themselves. A coach helps you come to your own answers.

As Oprah Winfrey so aptly put it, 'Make the strongest voice in your life your own.'

No one else can possibly know what is right for you. It is up to you to make decisions about your life. Ignore the well-meaning advice of others. Remember that this is *your* life.

I don't care what your neighbour or your best friend thinks is best for you. I am not interested in what job your parents always thought you should do. The only opinion that matters here is yours.

You can only ever make the best choice you can, at any point in time

All you can ever do is make the best decision you can at any point in time. Sure, you may choose an option and in a few months' time, with more information or experience at your disposal, you may realise you need to explore another option — so what? I personally believe that sometimes we have to go part of the way down different roads to learn that which we are supposed to learn. Be prepared to cut yourself some slack and accept that the decisions you make today may or may not need to change over time. Take the pressure off yourself. Try to make the best decisions you can, based on what you know and feel at this point in time. Don't hold off waiting for absolute certainty or clarity. Chances are that absolute certainty or clarity will never come.

The fear of making a wrong decision is a key reason that so many people are suffering from the Waiting Epidemic. 'But what if I get it wrong?' Too often, people are so afraid of making the wrong decision, they don't make any decision. They wait until they'll 'know for sure'.

> *'When faced with two equally tough choices,*
> *most people choose the third choice:*
> *to not choose.'*
>
> – Jarod Kintz

This is understandable. In school we were conditioned to find or know the right answer, and there was usually just one. However, in the real world, I am not so sure this 'one right answer' model is always relevant. I am sure we could think of examples where there are right and wrong decisions — probably more so in the sense of what we, as a society, would generally consider as morally or legally right or wrong. For example, for most people stealing would be considered a wrong decision. However, in day-to-day decisions, I suggest there may not always be right or wrong options, just different ones. Sometimes there will be clear-cut options. Sometimes, an option may stand out as the one to be preferred, and another as less preferred. In those cases, the decision-making process is much easier.

But what about those situations in which there may be numerous options available and yet no one obvious right answer? How do you know which one to go for? How do you know which one is the right one? Next time you find yourself in this situation — as you may do in making decisions about what you want in life — I encourage you to play with the possibility that there may be more than one right choice available to you. Remind yourself that you can only ever make the best choice you can, at any point in time. And make a decision.

Whatever the outcome, you will handle it

Trust that you are capable of making good decisions for yourself — because you are! Remember the affirmation 'I can handle anything'? Trusting yourself to make decisions is a lot easier when you know you can handle anything that comes your way.

Reflective questions

THE SECRET TO KNOWING
WHAT YOU WANT IN LIFE

Are you ready to decide what you want? How do you know?

How does the thought of knowing what you want make you feel?

How does the thought of deciding what you want make you feel?

What will you gain from deciding what you want?

What will you lose from deciding what you want?

7

Five-step process

for deciding what you want in life

'Most people plan their vacations with better care than they plan their lives.'

– Jim Rohn

'It is never too late to be what you might have been.'

— George Eliot

The following diagram provides an overview of what is involved in clarifying what you want in life and making it happen, the process I will be sharing with you over the remainder of this book.

As you can see from the diagram, there are multiple elements involved in knowing what you want. The process

Process for knowing and having what you want in life

Step 1: GET TO KNOW YOURSELF	Practise the art of self-reflection
	Do more of the things that you enjoy
	Raise your standards

‖‖‖‖‖‖‖‖‖‖

MAKE IT HAPPEN

Step outside of your comfort zone

Act despite fear

Live a 'kick-arse life'

Achieve your goals

SET FABULOUS GOALS

Step 5: DECIDE WHAT YOU WANT	Think Big!
	Brainstorm ideas
	Pull together your responses
	Identify common themes
	Research options
	Make decisions!

Step 2:
IDENTIFY YOUR VALUES

Clarify who you are:

What are you naturally drawn to?

When are you most 'in your element'?

Step 3:
DISCOVER YOUR PASSIONS

Clarify what you are most passionate about:

What truly excites you?

What 'makes your heart sing'?

Step 4:
ASK YOURSELF THE RIGHT QUESTIONS

Consider 'What do I want?' in relation to each area of your life (jigsaw-piece approach)

Reflect on a series of prompt questions

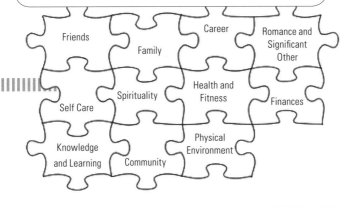

for knowing what you want can be broken down into five key steps. In the next five chapters, you will be taken through each of these steps. They are:

Step 1: Get to know yourself (Chapter 8)

Step 2: Identify your values (Chapter 9)

Step 3: Discover your passions (Chapter 10)

Step 4: Ask yourself the right questions (Chapter 11)

Step 5: Decide what you want (Chapter 12).

It makes sense that you must first be clear about *who* you are in order to be able to know *what* it is that you want for yourself. The process begins with a series of exercises for you to complete to facilitate your getting to know yourself better — accessing the information you already have within you. What matters most to you in life? What do you enjoy doing? What are you naturally drawn to? What most excites you?

You are then asked to consider the question 'What do I want for me?' in relation to each of the specific areas of your life, providing a multi-dimensional approach to considering what can otherwise be a very daunting question. You will also be asked to work through an extensive list of prompt questions, designed to help you further explore what you want for yourself in respect to the various areas of your life. When you are ready, you will take the information and insights gained and pull them altogether, explore various options, and ultimately, decide what you most want for yourself.

Once you have a clear picture of what you want, you will turn those ideas and intentions into specific goals and create clear action plans. Lastly, but all-importantly, the focus shifts to the specifics of making your goals happen.

Leave out any one of these steps, or approach them with any degree of half-heartedness (there's that attitude thing again), and your ability to successfully identify what you want in life will be jeopardised. In contrast, complete these steps with determination to know what you want for yourself, and respond to the exercises fully, and I am confident you will be well rewarded.

Why this process works

The process for deciding what you want in life isn't a perfect science. There is no one right process. I am sure an internet search would corroborate that. All I know is that the process I am about to share with you works. There are two reasons that this process is so effective.

First, it works because it is multi-dimensional. It relies on you completing numerous exercises, all quite different, and yet all focused on helping you access the information you have within you. There is always benefit in coming to any problem or issue from multiple perspectives or angles — some will inevitably be more effective for you than others (we are all different), but you will almost certainly gain more information if you look at something from multiple angles, than if you were to adopt a single, more narrowly focused approach.

Second, this process works because of the jigsaw-piece approach upon which it is based. Too often, in trying to clarify what we want in life, we do so from a whole-of-life perspective. We expect that we *should* know what it is that we want, and yet 'What do I want?' is such a huge, often overwhelming question. How do you even begin to answer it? This process works because it provides an alternative, more manageable — and thus, more effective — way in to knowing what you want, one piece at a time (as described below).

The 'jigsaw-piece approach' to clarifying what you want

When clients come to me asking for help in clarifying what they want, the first thing I do is encourage them to stop looking for or expecting to find 'the answer' to the question, 'What do I want (for my life)?' Why? Because it's a huge question and there is no one answer. No wonder it's so easy to answer, 'I don't know'.

I advocate a different approach.

Rather than considering 'What do I want (for my life)?', I encourage you to consider the question — not in relation to your life as a whole — but in relation to the various aspects of your life, one at a time. For example:

> ❯ 'What do I want for me in relation to my health and well-being/fitness?'

> ❯ 'What do I want my finances to look like?'

> ❯ 'What do I want my physical environment to be like?'

Breaking your planning and goal setting down in this way enables you to get to your 'What do I want?' answers with greater ease, making the task of clarifying what you want far more manageable and less daunting. It provides a structure for your thinking.

I often use the analogy of a jigsaw puzzle. Think of the various aspects of your life as jigsaw-puzzle pieces. Only when all of the jigsaw pieces are placed together do they form the whole, and enable you to see the complete picture. And so it is, too, with gaining clarity on what you want. Once you know what you want with respect to each of the various aspects of your life, all those pieces of information will, when put together, give you a complete picture of what you want for your life.

Before you begin …

Before you begin to work through the five-step process to clarify what you want, I encourage you to take a few moments to set up a framework for the work ahead. This will help provide both a structure for your thinking and a way to effectively organise and capture those thoughts.

Identify the various aspects of your life

I invite you to begin by considering the various aspects in your life (or pieces of your jigsaw). Look at the diagram below. We are all different, so perhaps some of these areas don't feature in your life, or you may think of others you would add to make your own list.

Life areas

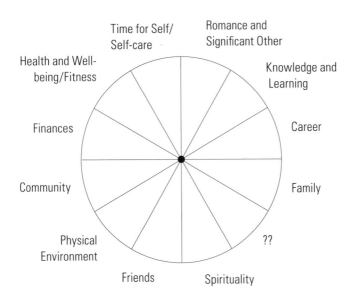

Create a list of the various areas of your life. You will be asked to come back to this list, repeatedly, while working through the coming chapters. As already mentioned, this list will provide a framework for you to consider and record your responses to the many exercises to come.

Create a template for recording your thoughts

Once you have your life list written down, take your book or journal, or create a new electronic document. Begin by writing your first life area at the top of a page. Allow a minimum of four pages, then write your second life area at the top of that page, and so on, until you have set up your book or document allowing plenty of writing space for each of the life areas you identified in the preceding exercise. You now have a template for capturing your ideas and thoughts, as you work through the exercises in the following chapters.

Step 1:
Get to know
yourself

'Knowing yourself is the beginning of all wisdom.'

— Aristotle

Before you begin any task it is important to be as ready as possible. The task of identifying what you want in life is no different. You need to be prepared.

Let's take the analogy of driving a car. What happens if you decide to drive a car but you don't have the car keys? Nothing! If the car is locked, you won't even be able to get into the car, let alone start the engine. Ensuring you have your car keys is a vital step in preparing to travel by car. If you think about it, many of our everyday tasks have prerequisites of some kind: a something (or several things) you need to do first, in order to be able to perform a task correctly.

And so it is, too, when it comes to clarifying what you want in life. Often people will come to me having almost given up on being able to clarify what they want for themselves. Yet as I talk to them, it becomes clear to me that they aren't ready to be able to easily identify what they want. They aren't prepared.

> You need to know the *who* (who you are) before you can possibly know the *what* (what you want).

So often people have grand expectations that they should be able to identify *what* they want — yet they have no knowledge of *who* they are, or at best very limited knowledge.

'If you don't go within, you'll go without.'

— Neale Donald Walsch

These days most people live such busy, full-on lives, they move from one task to the next, spending little, if any, time just 'being'. It is no wonder that people become disconnected with who they are. Being able to identify what we want in life requires us to stop. We need to stop being so busy and allow ourselves to become reacquainted with the person inside. Self-knowledge will make the process of clarifying what you want considerably easier.

> You do not get to know yourself simply by growing up and getting older. Knowing yourself requires conscious effort.

Strengthen your self-knowledge

No matter what level you would assess your current sense of self to be, I strongly encourage you to take the time to complete the exercises in this chapter. The insights you will gain will be vital in preparing you for the task of clarifying what you want for yourself during the course of the following chapters. Please don't be tempted to take a short cut. In my experience there is no such thing as an effective short cut when it comes to personal development.

There are three key aspects to strengthening your self-knowledge:

1. Practise the art of quiet self-reflection.

2. Do more of the things you enjoy.

3. Raise your standards.

Let's take a closer look at each of these.

1. Practise the art of quiet self-reflection

When was the last time you took time out of your busy life and your hectic schedule to do some self-reflection?

This involves creating quiet space, an environment with no interruptions, where you can clarify your thoughts by listening to your internal dialogue. This is where you get to stop being so busy, stop 'doing', and instead practise the art of 'just being'. It's where you connect with your inner voice, and where you get to focus on what your inner voice is telling you; on what you are thinking, and on how you are feeling. Self-reflection allows you to understand yourself more intimately.

> *'Put your ear down close to your soul*
> *and listen hard.'*
>
> — Anne Sexton

It may be challenging at first. Most people are completely out of practice at having quiet time by themselves. In fact, some people deliberately go out of their way to avoid it.

Being able to sit in your own company, comfortably, is key to being able to identify what you want for yourself — a task that will require considerable solitude, thought and self-reflection.

Self-reflection

Set aside at least 15 minutes each day, starting today, to 'just be'. This exercise will help grow your self-awareness and accustom you to the practice of 'going within' and reflecting on exactly where you are at.

I have included a list of some of my favourite questions to help focus your thinking, initially at least. Some of these will resonate with you more than others. That's fine. Think of these as merely a starting point. Enjoy the process of becoming better acquainted with yourself. It may feel a little strange or forced to begin with, but stick with it. New habits generally take 21 days to form, so don't expect this will feel normal straight away.

As you consider each question, I encourage you to write down whatever comes to mind. Keep your responses to these questions separate from the section you have already set up using your life areas as headings. Don't edit your thoughts. At this stage it is far more important that you simply capture them. Editing or analysing comes later. You will be amazed how some of the thoughts you have written off as unimportant actually end up being quite significant.

Reflective questions

What do you love to do?

What matters most to you in life?

What makes you happiest in your life?

What are you good at? What are your three greatest strengths?

What are you most grateful for?

What has been the most defining moment of your life?

What is missing from your life?

What opportunities are available to you right now?

When do you feel most like yourself?

What are you most proud of about your life?

What are your top three achievements?

What are you currently tolerating or putting up with?

What do you want more of in your life?

What do you want less of in your life?

What would make the biggest positive difference in your life right now?

How are you pursuing your dreams right now?

What do you most like about yourself?

In my experience, the questions people tend to find most difficult to answer are those relating to their strengths and their achievements. Keep focusing on these — don't give up just because the answers may take a little time.

2. Do more of the things you enjoy

It never ceases to astound me how little time people spend doing the things they enjoy.

> *'If life is so short, why do we do so many things*
> *that we don't like and like so many things*
> *that we don't do?'*
>
> — Author unknown

Doing things that you enjoy is a crucial part of looking after yourself, being happy and healthy, and feeling good. This is why any life-planning work I do always begins with at least one session on self-care, during which the clients' sole focus is identifying things they enjoy doing, and doing them. When initially given this exercise, the majority of people struggle to identify what they enjoy — it's often been such a long time! Yet, give them permission to make this a priority, and the tools and encouragement to make this happen, and this exercise alone can have a huge impact on how a person feels. Seriously.

Doing more of the things that give you pleasure will make you feel great, and you will be sending yourself an important message: 'I matter!' Because you do matter, yet that is something you can easily lose sight of in the busy-ness of day-to-day life.

Selfish versus selfless

If you are out of the habit of doing things for yourself, it can be challenging to begin honouring your own needs. Initially you may feel quite uncomfortable. You may even feel quite selfish.

Take a moment to consider what being selfish actually means. Selfishness occurs when you put your own needs ahead of someone else's, to the detriment of other people. What if you could take care of your own needs by doing more of the things you enjoy, with no detrimental impact on others? Surely this isn't selfish? It's just good, sensible self-care.

At the other end of the continuum is 'selflessness'. This is where many new clients are when they first start having coaching sessions. They frequently put everyone else's needs ahead of their own, to the detriment of themselves. For a short period of time this might be manageable, but not over the long term. No one can give tirelessly to others, to the detriment of their own needs, without something having to 'give' at some point.

When I talk about self-care in my workshops, I often use the analogy of being on an aeroplane. I am sure you will be familiar with the typical safety message they give prior to take-off: ' ... those of you travelling with young children, please make sure that, in the event of an emergency, you place your own mask on your face before attempting to help those you are travelling with.' Why is this instruction given? Why is it so important? The point here is clear: in the context of an aeroplane disaster, unless you take care of yourself you would be unable to take care of anyone else. And so it is in life. If we continue to put our own needs on the back-burner for too long, we compromise our ability to give as much of ourselves as we would like to others. In this respect, your own self-care is not only good for you as an individual, but it will also be of benefit to your family and friends. (I am sure my husband would testify to the fact that I am a much happier, more fun person to be around when I am looking after myself as well as him and our four children.)

I actually believe (adamantly) that it is far more selfish NOT to take care of yourself. Think about it. Consider your current state of health — in terms of physical, psychological and emotional well-being. Are you at your best? Is your current health enabling you to be the best you could be? Are you giving the best of yourself to your family and friends? Surely they also deserve to have the best 'you' that you can be.

Self-care is not selfish. It is common sense.

Things you enjoy

I encourage you to begin by writing down a list of things that give you pleasure. When you have written down as many as you can think of, keep going! I initially ask clients to aim for twenty items. Once they get to twenty, I ask them to double it! You will be amazed how many ideas you can think of when you get into the flow of this exercise. Often it's the simplest things in life that give us the greatest pleasure, like taking a bath, going for a walk or, corny as it may sound, taking time to stop and smell the roses. I have given you some ideas below in the hope that they may prompt your own thinking. We are all different, and gain pleasure from different things. Focus on identifying what 'does it' *for you*. Once you have your initial list, feel free to keep coming back to it and adding more items as they occur to you.

'Things I enjoy' ideas list

Walk / exercise	Try out a new hobby or sport
Listen to your favourite music	Be in nature (beach, bush, etc.)
Take a bath (perhaps even during the day)	Have fresh flowers in the house
Catch up with friends	Dance – by yourself!
Enjoy your favourite drink or food	Take 'time out' to do nothing at all
'Potter' in the garden	Watch your favourite movie
Read	Sit in the sunshine
Take the phone off the hook	Be creative (crafts, painting, etc.)
Say 'no' more often	Treat yourself to an ice cream (just because)
Get a facial, pedicure, etc.	
Visit an art gallery or museum	Smile a lot

Let me share with you a few items from my own list:

Flowers   I always have fresh flowers in the house. Whether I treat myself to a bouquet from the local florist shop or simply pick a small bunch from my own garden, flowers give me a lift. They make me smile. There is a vase of stunning red gerberas and orchids sitting on my desk as I type this. Just beautiful!

Exercise   Dancing competitively gives me a good incentive to train every day, whether it be fitness work or practising my routines. Dancing makes me feel alive.

The beach   I am blessed to live close to the beach. The clarity I can gain from even the shortest of walks along the beach never ceases to amaze me. There is something about it — the sand under my feet, the sound of the waves — that has the power to restore me to my calmer, more rational self, on even the busiest, most hectic of days. For me, time spent at the beach is heavenly.

My work environment   I have created a gorgeous, soul-nurturing work space in our home. I have a large desk from which I overlook the garden. Bi-fold doors open and allow me to feel as though I am working outside during the summer months, and an open fire keeps me cosy on colder days. I am also surrounded by things I love: family photos, my favourite books, gorgeous artwork and inspiring quotes. I never cease to appreciate being able to work in what really is a 'perfect-for-me' environment. It is definitely something I consciously enjoy every day.

A quiet glass of wine   When the day's myriad of children's after-school activities are over, and I am at home cooking dinner, I treat myself to a glass of my favourite pinot gris. It's another little thing I do, for me.

As you can see, things that give you pleasure needn't cost a lot of money, if any, nor need they be time-consuming. Some do cost money and definitely take time. But I encourage you to ensure you also identify plenty of things you enjoy that don't require any money and that take very little time, as these will be relatively easy for you to include in your lifestyle.

Now what? Start incorporating items from your list into your day. In other words, start doing more of the things you enjoy, things that give you pleasure — just because you deserve to!

How many items you choose to do each day is up to you. The number I suggest to clients varies greatly, depending on the person. If doing things for yourself is a completely foreign concept at present, then doing only two or three things a day from your list may seem huge. Yet if someone is used to doing things they enjoy, it might be more appropriate to challenge them to double their current level of self-care. You make the call. The key point is that you significantly increase the number of things you currently do that you enjoy — and not just occasionally, or on the weekends, but *every* day. You will be a 'happier you' as a consequence!

3. Raise your standards

I encourage you to go beyond making the conscious effort to do more of the things you enjoy, and, in addition, start treating yourself better in general. Make more of an effort with yourself. This is likely to involve raising your standards. You might choose to start dressing smarter, to de-clutter your home or even to spring-clean your friends (you know the ones I'm talking about — those who leave you feeling heavy or flat).

Think about your current level of effort with respect to your self-care and the environment in which you live. What messages are you sending to yourself?

It is amazing what a difference you will feel when you start treating yourself as though you matter. And don't be surprised if others around you also start treating you better as a consequence.

Choose to up your game
Take time to identify the areas in your life in which you could up your game, and ways in which you could start

taking the best possible care of yourself. Such areas might include:

> your appearance, your chosen look

> your health and well-being

> the physical environments in which you live and work

> your relationships with friends and family.

I also encourage you to consider the following questions:

> Are there some obvious opportunities here for you to raise the bar, simply because you deserve to?

> What are you currently tolerating that you could deal with instead?

> What unfinished task(s) could be completed?

> Could you benefit from starting to say 'no' to people? To whom in particular?

> What one action could you take right now that would make the biggest difference in each of the areas outlined above — your appearance, your health ...?

Write down everything that comes to mind — then take action. You'll be able to complete and tick off some of the items on your list relatively quickly. Other items may require considerable effort over a period of time. Keep acting on your list. Although not all of the tasks on your list will be fun (cleaning out one's pantry or ending a draining friendship are never going to be joyful activities), I'm sure you will be well rewarded for doing them.

Think about what you already know. For example, if you know that coming home to an unmade bed each day irritates you, make a new rule that from now on you will always make the bed as soon as you get up each morning.

If you know that you feel more confident and better about yourself when you make more of an effort getting ready in the morning, start allowing yourself an extra ten minutes to get dressed or do your hair and/or make-up.

I am sure you will quickly be able to identify opportunities to up your game. Start treating yourself with the care and respect you deserve.

Before you turn to the next chapter ...

Have you fully completed the exercises in this chapter? Be honest with yourself.

As I have already said, it makes sense that to be able to be clear about *what* you want in life, you first need to be clear about *who* you are as a person. This requires investing time in yourself. The stronger your sense of self, the more easily you will be able to complete the exercises contained in the following chapters. If you need to stop reading at this point until you have fully completed the exercises in this chapter, I strongly encourage you to do so. I realise there is often the temptation when reading a book such as this one, to keep ploughing on regardless of what is being asked of you along the way. However, please take the time you need to ensure you are as 'well positioned' as possible to clarify what you want. Remember: the car won't start without the keys!

Reflective questions

STEP 1:
GET TO KNOW YOURSELF

What insights did you gain (about yourself), from reflecting on the wisdom questions, that may have surprised you?

How does it feel now to be doing more things you enjoy, each day? What difference has this made?

In what ways are you now treating yourself better? What impact is this having on how you feel?

In which aspects of getting to know yourself could you up your game further? What are you going to do about it?

9

Step 2: Identify your values

'Your vision will become clear only when you look inside your own heart. Who looks outside, dreams; who looks inside, awakens.'

— Carl Jung

I am about to share with you the programme I designed to assist clients discover their core values.

Let me explain what I mean by values. In this context, values are the behaviours or activities towards which you are naturally drawn. When engaged in these activities, you find them seemingly effortless. You feel in your element, happy and connected. Your core values represent the very essence of who you are.

When you understand your values, a direction begins to

become clear, and you have a solid basis on which to make decisions about what you want in life.

Let me share something of my past to illustrate what a powerful difference aligning your life to your values makes. You may be able to relate to aspects of my story.

When I first joined the workforce I had just completed my tertiary studies, and a number of organisations were promoting graduate recruitment programmes. Positions on such programmes were highly sought after. They provided new graduates with the opportunity to fast-track their careers, and offered great starting packages. Although none of the organisations were directly related to my area of interest (psychology), I applied. What did I have to lose? I was offered a position. By all accounts it was a great opportunity. Within six months I found myself in a specialist role within National Office. Within three years I was in a senior advisory role, working on an array of high-profile projects. I met some amazing people. And I was well remunerated. I *should* have been very happy. But while there were many aspects of my role I did enjoy, I knew I wasn't doing the work I was here to do. As I have already shared with you, I wanted 'more'. I wanted to do something that made a real, positive difference to the lives of others — something that I felt truly mattered.

It was only as I delved further into the area of personal development that I came to understand why I had felt as I did. Finally it made sense why my 'perfectly good job' simply didn't 'do it' for me. The work I was doing was incongruent with my personal values.

My key values (which I didn't know back then, but certainly do now) are: (to) inspire; (to be a) catalyst; (to be) connected; (to) achieve and (to have) passion. It's no wonder writing ministerial reports and strategic plans didn't 'feed me'. Fast-forward several years to the present — and I absolutely love the work I do now. Through my coaching, writing and speaking I connect/engage with extraordinary people, in an environment in which I have their permission to challenge them and inspire personal change. I am passionate about what I do. And I feed off the passion I see in others as they also create fulfilling lives. My work also gives me a sense of achievement, of making a real difference. I'm finally doing work that truly matters to me.

See what a difference it made when I realigned my work to my values? I want this for you too, with respect to every area of your life. A life aligned to your values will naturally feed you, give you pleasure, and enable you to be at your best. It makes sense, then, that identifying your core values is a key aspect of clarifying what you want in your life.

Identify your core values

This exercise will help you identify your top five values.

The following list contains 200 possible values. A value is a must for you to be yourself. Taking your time, work through the list and note those that resonate with you in some way. Write these down. It is likely that some words will seem to jump out at you, and just feel right. Also notice any words that you may feel you are resisting. Sometimes such words can refer to hidden values that we haven't previously recognised as being important to us, or it may be that you are resisting the idea of a certain value because the thought of aligning your life to reflect that value simply feels too big. In addition, be careful not to choose any words that you consider *should* be a value. If the value word doesn't speak to you, it's not one of your core values.

Once you have worked through this list and identified the words in it that resonate with you, add any other words or phrases that you feel are important to you and that you would like to include. Words can mean different things to different people, and thus it's important that you find the right word for you. If there is another word that reflects more closely what matters most to you, add it to your list. You have free licence here to add, change or replace these words with whatever words feel most right to you. In this context, semantics are incredibly important.

Abundance
Accomplish
Accountability
Achieve
Adventure
Affection
Alter
Arouse
Assert
Assist
Attractiveness
Authenticity
Autonomy

Beauty
Being the best
Belonging

Calmness
Carefulness
Catalyst
Cause
Certainty
Challenge
Co-operation
Coach
Collaboration
Commitment
Communication
Community
Compassion
Competence

Competitiveness
Connection
Consensus
Consistency
Contentment
Continuous improvement
Contribution
Control
Courage
Creativity

Danger
Dare
Decadence
Decisiveness
Dedication
Democracy
Design
Determination
Discipline
Discovery
Dominate field
Duty

Education
Effectiveness
Elegance
Empathy
Encouragement
Energise
Engage
Entertain

Equality
Excellence
Excitement
Experiment
Expertise
Explain
Exploration
Expressiveness

Fairness
Faith
Family
Fellowship
Flexibility
Flow
Freedom
Fun

Glamour
Govern
Grace
Gratitude
Guidance

Harmony
Healing
Holiness
Honesty
Hope
Humour
Imagination
Impact
Improve
Inclusiveness
Independence
Influence
Ingenuity
Innovate
Inquisitiveness
Insightfulness

Inspire
Integrity
Intelligence
Intuition
Invent
Involvement

Joy
Justice

Knowledge

Leadership
Learning
Love
Loyalty
Luxury

Magnificence
Making a difference
Mastery
Mentor
Motivation
Move forward
Nomadic
Nurture

Open-mindedness
Optimism
Order
Originality
Outdo
Ownership

Partnership
Passion
Peace
Perform
Persuade
Philanthropy

Plan
Play
Pleasure
Possibility
Preparedness
Professionalism
Protection
Provide

Quality

Radiance
Rebelliousness
Recognition
Refinement
Reliability
Religious
Responsibility
Responsiveness
Results-orientated
Rigour
Risk
Rule field

Safety
Security
Self-awareness
Self-reliance
Sensitivity
Sensuality
Serenity
Service
Sexuality
Sharing
Shrewdness
Significance
Simplicity
Solitude

Solutions-focused
Spark
Be spiritual
Spontaneity
Stability
Status
Stimulate
Strategic
Strength
Structure
Style
Success
Superiority
Support

Teach
Teamwork
Thoroughness
Thoughtfulness
Thrill
Tolerance
Tradition
Trust
Turn on

Understanding
Uniqueness
Unity
The unknown
Usefulness

Victory
Vision
Voice

Wealth
Wild
Win

How many values have you identified? At this stage, I ask you to narrow your list down to a maximum of ten items. Review each word and identify the ten that feel most important to you. I know this can be challenging given the length of the list, but keep working through it. (If you have fewer than ten, that's fine.)

Identify your top five values

Now it's time to reduce your top ten to your top five. Which five values are the most important of all? You may know immediately. Or you may not. If this is a little difficult, consider whether there are any obvious groupings of values within your top ten. For example, if you have chosen both 'accomplish' and 'achieve' you might decide on 'accomplish' if, for you, this also encapsulates the value 'achieve'. Reducing your top ten to your top five is a very personal task because only you can know what a certain word means to you, the emotional reaction it generates within you, and the relative strength of those reactions.

It can be helpful to write a brief definition or description of what each value means to you. A single sentence is sufficient. What does that value actually mean to you? What comes to mind when you think of it? Using my own values as examples, to me 'inspire' is about challenging others' thinking in a way that leaves them seeking more for themselves. Another of my values is 'passion'. To me, 'passion' is about choosing to fully embrace and commit myself to everything I do. As you can see, values definitions needn't be complex. Just aim to write a simple statement of what each of your values means to you.

I often get my clients to talk me through each of their top ten values. As they describe each one, and what each word actually means to them, it's amazing how quickly they are able to clarify which are most important to them.

If you are a more visual person, you may prefer to find an image or a collection of images to represent what each of your values mean to you. (Google Images and Pinterest are great sources of pictures to assist with this task.) Finding the 'right image' can be an incredibly powerful way to express what a given value means to you and the feelings you associate with it.

Whether you choose to write a definition or to find an appropriate image as your way of clarifying the specific nature of each of your values, stay conscious of how each value makes you feel. Which values most excite you? Which values make you smile? Which simply feel most 'you'?

Keep comparing each value word against the others, until you have a shortlist of your five personal values that totally, absolutely, definitely, are 100 per cent reflective of who you are and what's most important to you. You will know when you have successfully completed this exercise because your chosen top five will 'feel right'.

Create your value-based 'picture'

Now that you have identified your top five values, and you have a distinct, very specific understanding of what each one means for you, it is time to clarify what a life based on living those values might look like.

Use your list of life areas to help you do this. Open your exercise book, journal or file to where you set aside pages headed up for each of the various aspects of your life.

Look at the first of your five values and consider this in relation to each aspect of your life. Ask yourself, 'How might I express this value in this area of my life?'

Overlay of each of your five key values with each area of your life

LIFE AREAS

Health and Well-being/Fitness

Time for Self/Self-care

Romance and Significant Other

Career

Family

Knowledge and Learning

Spirituality

Friends

Physical Environment

Community

Finances

YOUR FIVE KEY VALUES

VALUE 1

'How might I express this value in each area of my life?'

VALUE 2

'How might I express this value in each area of my life?'

VALUE 3

'How might I express this value in each area of my life?'

VALUE 4

'How might I express this value in each area of my life?'

VALUE 5

'How might I express this value in each area of my life?'

Expressing your values in your life

Take the time to fully consider the following questions as well, with respect to each value/life-area combination. These questions may spark other thoughts as you look to identify ways in which you can express your values in the various areas of your life. Write down all of your ideas.

Consider:

> To what extent is this value expressed in this area of your life at present?

> How could this value be more fully expressed in this area of your life?

> What changes could you make in your life in order to *fully* honour and express this value in this area of your life?

> What project or goal could you design (with respect to this area of your life) that would allow you to express this value?

Have fun with this exercise. Play with it a little. Let your imagination go, don't edit your thoughts, just record them. And remember to think big. The bigger the better! You are not being asked to commit to these changes, you are simply being encouraged to explore possibilities at this stage. This is a brainstorming exercise.

Let's look at some examples.

> A value of 'to achieve' in the area of health and well-being/fitness might translate to running a marathon, making the national (or local) team (in your chosen sport) or — for a non-swimmer — learning to swim.

> With respect to finances, 'to achieve' could translate to make a million dollars by the end of this year, become debt free or save $10,000 for a family holiday.

> ❭ With respect to the area of career, 'to achieve' could include writing a book, doubling my client base in the next three months or starting my own business.

I could ask a group of ten people with the same values to complete this exercise and, chances are, they would each identify quite different ways in which they would choose to express those same values. The key is to focus in on what each of your top five values means *to you*, and what your own expression of those values could look and feel like.

Take your time. You are being asked to consider each of your five values in relation to each of the various aspects of your life. In my case that's 55 value/life-area combinations to consider and it's likely that your number will be similar. If during the course of this exercise you feel yourself losing focus, take a break and come back to it when you feel refreshed. You want to be at your most creative with this task. You are also likely to find that ideas come to you even when you are doing other things. Write them down and add them to your list. Keep building your picture of what a life based on your values might or could include.

10

Step 3: Discover your passions

'Only passions, great passions can elevate the soul to great things.'

— Denis Diderot

Imagine waking each morning truly excited about what the day ahead holds. Imagine feeling so engaged in what you are doing that time passes effortlessly, you are totally in the moment and loving it — each and every day. This is what's possible when you live your passions.

For me, passions can best be described as those things that make you come alive. My number-one passion (other than my family, of course) is dancing. At the ripe old age of 40-something, I still do competitive ballroom and Latin

American dancing. I absolutely love it. I am in my element when I feel I am dancing at my best. It keeps me fit, it keeps me goal-focused and I get to travel nationally and internationally, doing what I most love to do.

So often people who can see the love I have for dancing comment on how 'lucky' I am to have it — as though I have won some lottery, or am part of a 'select few' fortunate enough to be able to pursue a passion. I am definitely fortunate to have an amazing husband who is so supportive of my dancing. I am lucky in that respect, yes. But I am not dancing because I am lucky. I am dancing because I know what I am passionate about and I choose to pursue that passion. It's not about luck. It's about choice. Anyone can have their own equivalent of my dancing.

Living your passions is phenomenal. And yet I believe the majority of people are clueless as to what their passions are. They wonder why their lives lack a sustainable sense of joy. What are you most passionate about in life? What really gets you excited? What do you most love to do with your time? What makes you feel unstoppable? Which activities make you lose track of time?

Identify your passions

The following exercises are among those I share with clients seeking to clarify their passions. These are designed to help you identify your passions from a variety of different angles. I encourage you to complete all of the exercises. Keep a record of all the thoughts and ideas these exercises generate, whether or not you think they are worth recording.

Once you have completed all the exercises, we will look at how you can use the insights you have gained and pull all of the information you have gathered together, in order to identify your shortlist of passions.

1. Six months to go

If you had only six months to live – what would you do? How would you spend your time?

2. Freedom to choose

If you won $50 million and had complete freedom to choose, how would you spend your time? Identifying what you would be naturally drawn to, if money was not an issue, can be very revealing.

3. Lifelong dream

What have you always wanted to do but been afraid of? Is there something you have always planned to do 'one day'? What is your 'one day' goal? What perhaps previously seemingly unobtainable goal has always excited you?

4. The things that excite you

What activities completely inspire or excite you, light you up or give you the greatest pleasure? List every item that comes to mind. These might include travel, style, art, beauty, nature, adventure, the pursuit of understanding, creating possibilities, ground-breaking thinking, instituting change, making sushi, great wine, trying new things, working with your hands – list whatever it is that excites you.

5. The best of times

Think back to the three best periods of your life. These will be intervals, times or experiences when you felt the highest degree of satisfaction and fulfilment and achieved the best results. What was it about these times that gave you so much happiness and pleasure? What did they have in common? Note the qualities of experience that were present at the time. What is it about yourself that responded so favourably to these three experiences?

6. Looking for lifelong patterns

Search back into memories of your childhood. What did you always want to be? What did you love to do? What kinds of things excited you? What did you dream or fantasise about as a child? Is there something you loved to do back then that you still love to do today?

It is not uncommon for us, as adults, to have difficulty remembering much from our childhood. One way of answering these questions is to ask the people you grew up with ... your parents, siblings, friends, etc. You may be surprised by the things they remind you about.

7. Just one wish

Imagine you had a magic wand and could reinvent any part of your life from the beginning. What change would you make? What would you do differently?

8. That 'feel-good' factor

What gives you the greatest feeling of mental well-being, self-esteem and self-worth? What are you doing when you are feeling at your best? What activities give you that feel-good experience?

9. Your favourite three movies

Without over-thinking this, list your favourite three movies. What's the common thread that runs through them? How might this common thread reflect your own passions?

10. Your preferred reading material

What is your favourite section in a book shop? What magazines and blogs do you most enjoy reading?

11. Ask around

Ask 15 people you know what work or career they can see you in, and why.

Treat this as a survey – do not judge or critique what they say, just note it all down, then go back and look for any common threads.

12. Losing track of time

Pay attention to moments when you lose track of time, when you are completely absorbed by the task at hand. What you are doing at those moments? Whom are you surrounded by?

13. Your strengths

When do you consistently work or perform beyond reasonable expectations? Make a list. Often we perform best in the areas that we most enjoy. Consider whether the areas or activities on your list hold any clues as to what you are most passionate about.

Identify your top five passions

Now that you have completed the exercises, take a step back and look at your responses to them. Identify any common ideas or themes that have been revealed. What can you learn from the information in front of you? What insights can you gain?

Create a list of your passions. From this, identify your top five passions — the five areas that bring you most joy and excite you most.

Keep reviewing your answers to the exercises and revisiting your shortlist of passions until you are completely satisfied that those you have selected do, in fact, represent the things in life that most excite you.

Looking at your list of identified passions, how do you feel about these? Do they feel right?

Once you are satisfied with your 'top five', look to better understand the specific nature of each of your passions, just as you did in the values exercise.

What is it about each passion that most excites you? If, for example, you have a passion for teaching, what subject do you most enjoy teaching, and to whom? What specifically is it about teaching that you are so passionate about? If you have a passion for people, is your passion about helping others, entertaining others, teaching others, inspiring others, connecting with others ... ? If you have a passion for helping others, what do you most enjoy helping others do, and how specifically do you do that?

Once again, if you are a more visual person, you may prefer to find an image or a collection of images that for you represents the specific nature of your passion. Grab a pile of magazines and a pair of scissors or search Google Images or Pinterest. It is amazing how powerful the right image can be.

Keep pushing yourself until you have a clear understanding of each of your five top passions. This will help you in the next part of this exercise.

Create your passion-based 'picture'

Now that you have identified your top five passions, it is time to explore what a life based on living those passions might look like.

Just as you did in the previous chapter with respect to your values, I encourage you to use your previously identified list of life areas to help you. Turn to the pages you have headed up for each of the areas of your life.

Look at the first of your five passions and consider this in relation to each aspect of your life. Ask yourself, 'How might I express this passion in this area of my life?'

In some cases you might draw a blank, and not be able to identify any correlation between your passion and that particular aspect of your life. That's fine. It's reasonable that your passions will be relevant to some aspects of your life, yet not at all to others. Where there is a link, be as creative and as specific as you can.

Overlay of each of your five top passions with each area of your life

LIFE AREAS

Health and Well-being/Fitness

Time for Self/Self-care

Romance and Significant Other

Career

Family

Knowledge and Learning

Spirituality

Friends

Physical Environment

Community

Finances

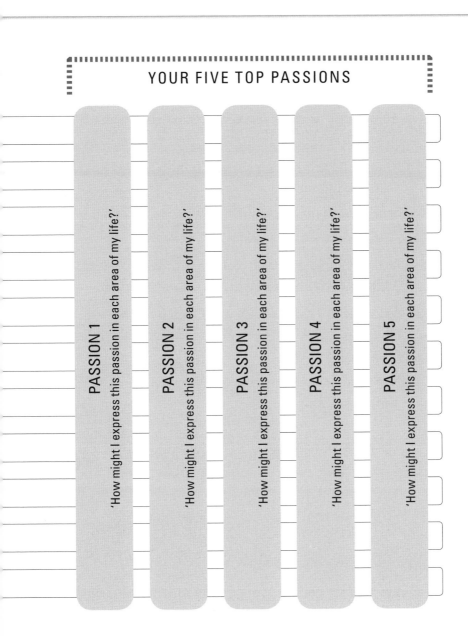

YOUR FIVE TOP PASSIONS

PASSION 1

'How might I express this passion in each area of my life?'

PASSION 2

'How might I express this passion in each area of my life?'

PASSION 3

'How might I express this passion in each area of my life?'

PASSION 4

'How might I express this passion in each area of my life?'

PASSION 5

'How might I express this passion in each area of my life?'

Expressing your passions in your life

Take the time to fully consider each of your five top passions, overlaid in this way against each of the various areas of your life. Record your answers and ideas. Consider the following questions with respect to each passion/life-area combination:

> How is this passion expressed in this area of your life at present?

> How could this passion be more fully expressed in this area of your life?

> What would living your life based on this passion look like with respect to this area of your life?

> What changes could you make in your life in order to fully indulge this passion in this area of your life?

> What project or goal could you design (with respect to this area of your life) that would allow you to fully indulge this passion?

> How else could you enjoy your passion with respect to this area of your life?

Have fun with this. Think of this as a brainstorming exercise. Be playful. Allow yourself to think outside the box. Simply write down whatever comes to mind. You will have plenty of opportunity to edit and critique your thoughts at a later stage.

Still not sure what your passions are?

In my experience the exercises above work well to help most people identify those things in life they feel most passionate about. However, it stands to reason that the exercises will not work if you have yet to experience those things that fill you with the joy and excitement that passions do. It is perfectly reasonable that you may not have encountered your areas of passion yet.

So, if at this point you genuinely can't identify your passions, then my advice to you is to go out and find them. This will involve stepping out of your comfort zone and trying new things, and continuing to do so until you discover something you are passionate about. I am passionate about dancing, something I may never have discovered unless I had given dancing a go. I began dancing at the age of ten, but stopped following the sudden death of my father two years later. Although I haven't always danced, that initial exposure to dancing had a significant impact on me. I knew it was something I enjoyed, something I wanted to do again 'one day'. If you are yet to find your passions, don't let this dishearten you, let it excite and motivate you to get out there and experience more of what life has to offer!

11

Step 4:
Ask yourself the
right questions

*'The key to wisdom is knowing
all the right questions.'*

— John Simone

That dreaded 'What do I want for me?' question ... one piece at a time

In Chapter 7, I encouraged you to stop looking for or expecting to find the answer to the 'What do I want for my life?' question, and to instead consider 'What do I want?' in relation to each of the different aspects of your life. Gaining clarity with respect to each aspect of your life (or one piece of the jigsaw puzzle at a time) is far more manageable, and when put together, these pieces allow you to see the whole picture — your completed jigsaw.

A multi-dimensional approach

This chapter takes you through two exercises designed to assist you clarify what you want for your life. It often helps to approach a task from more than one angle or perspective. Different approaches work more effectively for different people. Follow the directions given and complete all aspects of the exercises. Accept that some elements will be more helpful to you than others.

There are two distinct exercises to be completed as part of this step:

Exercise One: Answer the three key 'what' questions.

Exercise Two: Consider a set of prompt questions.

Record your answers to both of these exercises on the pages headed up in your journal or electronic document for each of your life areas.

Exercise One – Three key 'what' questions

I invite you to consider the following three 'what' questions, one at a time, with respect to each of the areas of your life:

> 'What do I want?'

> 'What do I NOT want?'

> 'What do I want instead?'

This isn't a two-minute exercise! This is an exercise that requires time and space: physical, mental and emotional space so that you can think, uninterrupted, with no distractions. It is also an exercise that I encourage you to complete over a period of time so that you can record your initial thoughts and responses, then come back to them once you have had the opportunity to reflect more fully. Perhaps you will set aside an hour a day for a week, or a couple of hours a day for the next few days.

Don't be surprised if ideas and thoughts come to you out of the blue when you least expect them, such as when you're getting your weekly groceries or driving to work! Once you start this process, your subconscious brain will continue to mull over the questions even when you're unaware you are doing so. It may pay to start carrying a pen and paper around with you.

Choose a life area to focus on first. It may be the first of the headings you wrote in your journal or document, but it doesn't necessarily need to be. Some categories will definitely be easier than others. In my experience, Health and Well-being/fitness is often a good starting point, but it's over to you.

Question One – 'What do I want?'

Ask yourself 'What do I want?' in relation to the life area you have chosen to focus on:

- 'What do I want in relation to my health and well-being/fitness?'

- 'What do I want in relation to my career?'

- 'What do I want for myself financially?'

- 'What do I want for myself …' in whatever aspect of your life you have chosen to focus on first.

Your gut response to this question may be to answer, 'I don't know'. And if you don't that's fine. But take the time to truly consider this question. Now that, perhaps for the first time, you are asking the 'What do I want?' question by life area, rather than for your life as a whole, you may surprise yourself when you discover just how much you do already know. It might be something big. It might be small. Whatever comes to mind, record it.

It might also be that while you don't know precisely what you want, you are able to describe some features of what you would like that unknown something to include or involve. For example, you may have no idea at this point about what you want to do in terms of a career, but you do know you want to work full-time, and preferably be self-employed. Great! Write that down. It's okay not to have the answer to the 'self-employed doing what?' question yet. At least you know something of what you want in relation to this area. Every little bit of information or clue is an important part of moving you closer to gaining the clarity you seek. Focus on what you *do* know, rather than what you *don't* know.

Only once you have completely exhausted your 'What do I want?' thinking with respect to that aspect, move on to the second 'what' question (for that same life area).

Question Two – 'What do I NOT want?'

Even if my clients claim not to know what they want, they can invariably tell me what they don't want! Knowing what you don't want is a great first step to clarifying what you *do* want. For example, it might be that you don't know what you want in relation to career/work, but you do know that you don't want to be stuck in an office all day. Great. Write that down. Take advantage of what you know you don't want. All knowledge is good and in this context, knowing what you don't want is highly useful in helping you identify what it is that you want instead.

Question Three – 'What do I want instead?'

Once you have your 'What I don't want' list, then ask yourself 'What do I want instead?' This is a great question. For everything that you know you don't want, ask 'What do I want instead?' Let's go back to the example of knowing you don't want to be stuck in an office. That's an important insight. From there, ask yourself, 'so what do I want instead?' Maybe you will find yourself saying, 'I want to work outside', or 'I'd love to be out on the road'. Write down whatever comes to you.

You will be amazed by the ideas and options that come to you when you ask yourself the right questions and when you are ready to find the answers. The key here is to keep drilling down, keep asking yourself the same questions over and over again if need be: 'What do I not want?' ... and so, 'What do I want instead?'

Exercise Two – Prompt questions

Once you feel you have exhausted your thinking using the three 'what' questions with respect to the area of your life you are focusing on, consider the 'prompt questions' given below.

As their name suggests, these questions are designed to prompt your thinking as you consider what you want for yourself. They provide an alternative means to accessing the information that I believe is already within you. Take your time. Don't rush. Reflect fully on each question and write down your answers. Questions can be incredibly powerful. Some will resonate with you more than others. Different questions will resonate with different people. Sometimes just asking yourself the right question can prompt you to identify thoughts or ideas that otherwise may not have come to you. These prompt questions are designed to complement the three 'what' questions you considered when completing Exercise One.

Although the questions are very specific to each of the different life areas, one question is asked in relation to all of the life areas. Included in the prompt questions for every life area is a question about whether you have a 'one day' goal. If this is a new term for you, a 'one day' goal is something that you have always thought you would like to have or do. 'One day I'm going to be my own boss.' 'One day I'm going to go back to university and finish my degree.' 'One day I'm going to go on a cruise around the Greek Islands.' Most people have 'one day' goals. I wonder what yours are? Recalling these can provide powerful insight into what you want in life.

Prompt questions

Health and Well-being/fitness

Record your answers to these questions on the pages in your journal or document headed 'Health and Well-being/fitness'.

- What would a healthier you look and feel like?

- What could you do to achieve a healthier you?

- What is the one change you could make that would have the biggest impact on your current health and well-being?

- What forms of exercise do you most enjoy?

- When was the last time you exercised? What did you do?

- What forms of exercise have you always wanted to try?

- What is the biggest, most exciting and most scary fitness goal you can think of?

- How do you want to feel about your body?

- What would you like to change about your physical appearance?

- How much do you weigh? How much would you like to weigh?

- In what way could you become physically healthier?

- In what way could you become emotionally healthier?

- Do you have a 'one day' goal in relation to your health and well-being/fitness? What is it?

Knowledge and Learning

Record your answers to these questions on the pages in your journal or document headed 'Knowledge and Learning'.

- What would you love to know how to do?

- What would you love to be really good at?

- What do you want to see that you haven't seen?

- What do you want to experience that you haven't experienced?

- What would you want to learn or achieve if you knew you could not fail?

- What do you want to do that you haven't done?

- What do you want to try that you haven't tried?

- What organisations or clubs interest you? Why aren't you already a member?

- Where would you like to travel to, that you haven't been to previously, and why would you like to go there?

- Is there something you have always thought you would like to learn or know one day?

Time for self / Self-care

Record your answers to these questions on the pages in your journal or document headed 'Time for self / Self-care'.

- What kinds of activities do you enjoy doing by yourself?

- Do you enjoy your own company? Why, or why not?

- If you truly knew you mattered, how would you reflect this in your self-care?

- What makes you happy?

- When did you last 'play'? What did you do?

- What do you do for fun?

- How could you have more fun in your life?

- How could you create more time for yourself?

- Do you have a 'one day' goal in relation to your self-care?
  What is it?

Finances
Record your answers to these questions on the pages in your journal or document headed 'Finances'.

- What does financial success look like to you?

- What do you want to accomplish financially?

- What is your strategy for increasing your savings/investments?

- How could you increase your income?

- How could you eliminate your debt?

- What is the one decision you could make that would have the most significant positive impact on your financial position?

- What is your financial 'one day' goal?

Romance and significant other
Record your answers to these questions on the pages in your journal or document headed 'Romance and significant other'.

- What would your 'ideal relationship' look and feel like?
  Describe it.

- How could you bring your existing relationship closer to the 'ideal' you have just described?

- What kinds of activities do you enjoy doing with your significant other?

- What's your definition of 'romantic'? Is romance important to you?

- What might deliberate, regular couple time look like?

- If you are currently in a relationship, is this person your soul-mate or your stop-gap?

- Do you have the relationship you deserve?

- In what ways could you grow your intimacy with your partner?

- What was it that first attracted you to your current partner? Do you still find this attractive?

- What do you enjoy most about your relationship?

- What do you feel you need more of from your partner?

- What might you need to give more of to your partner?

- Do you share the same values, enjoy the same interests as your partner?

- What joint goals do you have? What joint goals would you like to have as a couple?

- Ideally, how do you want to feel when you are with your partner? Is this how you do feel?

- If you are currently single, how do you feel about that?

- If you are currently single, what attributes would your 'ideal person' have? Where might you find this person?

- Do you have a 'one day' goal in respect of your relationship? What is it?

Spirituality

Record your answers to these questions on the pages in your journal or document headed 'Spirituality'.

- What does 'spirituality' mean to you?

- What is your 'spiritual path'?

- In what way would you like to grow spiritually?

- Do you have a 'one day' goal in your relation to your spirituality? What is it?

Friends

Record your answers to these questions on the pages in your journal or document headed 'Friends'.

- Describe your 'ideal friend' – what attributes would he/she have?

- What kinds of activities do you enjoy doing with friends?

- Who are your five closest friends? What is it about these people that you most enjoy and value?

- How do you feel when you are with your friends? Is this how you want to feel?

- When was the last time you spent time with your friends? What did you do?

- How could you foster your friendships with those who matter most to you? Identify specific actions you could take.

- How well do you manage your time socially?

- Knowing what you know now, is there any friendship that you would not start up again?

- What kind of friend are you? How might your friends describe you?

- Do you have a loyal circle of friends who support and energise you?

- When was the last time you made a new friend? Where did you meet him/her?

- If you chose to 'step up' your friendships, what would that look or feel like? What would it involve? What would change?

- Do you have a 'one day' goal in relation to your friendships? What is it?

Family

Record your answers to these questions on the pages in your journal or document headed 'Family'.

- What matters to you in terms of your family?

- How much time do you spend with your family?

- In spending time with your family, is the focus more on the quality or quantity of time?

- How do your family know that you love them?

- How do you feel when you are with your family? Is this how you want to feel?

- What kinds of activities do you enjoy doing with your family?

- What does (or could) deliberate, regular family time look like?

- What things would you like to be remembered for by those you are closest to? What legacy would you like to leave behind for them? How would you like your loved ones to describe you?

- In what ways would you like your children to grow emotionally, socially and spiritually? What might this require of you?

- Do you have a 'one day' goal in relation to your family? What is it?

Physical environment

Record your answers to these questions on the pages in your journal or document headed 'Physical environment'.

- How do you wish to feel in your environment? Is this how you actually feel?

- To what extent is your current living environment working for you? What works well? What could be improved/changed?

- What would your 'ideal' home look and feel like? What features would it include?

- To what extent is your current work environment working for you? What works well? What could be improved/ changed?

- What would your 'ideal' work environment look and feel like? What features would it include?

- What are you currently putting up with/tolerating in terms of your home and work environments? What could you do to address these issues? What impact would this have on how you currently feel?

- What possessions would you like to own? What needs to happen for you to be able to own these things?

- What is your 'one day' goal in relation to your physical environment?

Career

Record your answers to these questions on the pages in your journal or document headed 'Career'.

- Do you enjoy your current job? What do you most enjoy? What do you least enjoy?

- If you could have any occupation in the world, what would it be, and why would you choose that occupation?

- What other occupations really interest you?

- What is the work you simply can't NOT do?

- What do you want to achieve or accomplish in your career?

- What does success look like to you?

- Is there another kind of work you would rather be doing? If so, what is it?

- Are you making use of all of your strengths?

- When you were a child, what did you always want to be when you grew up?

- What matters most to you in terms of your career?

- What are you naturally good at? What is your special talent or gift?

- Do you regularly take time off work? When was the last time you had a holiday?

- What drives or motivates you within the work environment? For example, is it money, a sense of achievement, a sense of contribution ... ?

- What do you want to accomplish?

- What is effortless for you?

- If your current job ceased to exist, what sort of work would you choose to start over in? What industry interests you? Why?

- What features would exist in your ideal job (even if you're not sure what that ideal job is) – for example, would you work full-time or part-time? Would you work indoors or outdoors? If you would prefer to work inside, would that be in an office environment, or in some other environment? Would you like to travel as part of your role? Do you have any geographical preferences? List as many features as you can think of.

- What are your top five skills? If you're not sure, ask others who know you.

- Do you have a 'one day' goal in relation to your career? What is it?

Community

Record your answers to these questions on the pages in your journal or document headed 'Community'.

- How could you be of service to your immediate community?

- In what capacity could you volunteer?

- What difference do you want to make in the world?

- What contribution do you want to make to the world?

- Do you have a 'one day' goal in relation to community? What is it?

12

Step 5: Decide what you want

'The indispensible first step to getting the things you want out of life is this: decide what you want.'

— Ben Stein

This is where the real fun begins! Up to this point I have deliberately encouraged you to write down your thoughts and responses to the exercises, without editing or analysing them. It was important for you just to capture the core of what came to you. Now is the time to put your virtual analytical hat on and to look for the key insights and repeated themes within the information you have gathered.

From information gathering to decision making

In Chapter 6, I shared the somewhat less-than-profound secret to knowing what you want in life. Do you recall what that was? *Deciding* what you want. Knowing what you want in life ultimately requires that you decide what you want.

Assuming that you have completed all of the exercises set out in the preceding chapters, you now have a considerable amount of information available to you:

> Information about yourself — including what matters most to you, what you are good at and what you enjoy (Chapter 8).

> Your top five values (Chapter 9).

> Your top five passions (Chapter 10).

> Your answers to the three 'what' questions, for each life area (Chapter 11).

> Your answers to the prompt questions, for each life area (Chapter 11).

Your task now is to take all of that information and sift through it. This will help you determine the most relevant pieces, clarify what this information is telling you, identify common themes, analyse the various options, undertake any further research required, and from there, *decide what you want*.

Unfortunately, this part of the process is not so easily scripted. We are all individuals and each of us goes about the process of making a decision in our own unique way. Some people are highly analytical and cautious. Others are more intuitive and make decisions quickly. Whatever your decision-making style might be, this stage of the process is very much about finding your own answers within the information that you now have. Some people are more visual than others. Some are more auditory. Adapt this part of the process as you see fit.

As you begin to work through the decision-making process outlined below, I encourage you to keep in mind the 'truths' about decision-making we discussed in Chapter 6. These are certainly worth repeating. Let them guide you and give you confidence in your ability to make decisions about what you want for yourself. Let them empower you:

'Truths' about decision making

> You, and only you, can know what is right for you.
> You can only ever make the best choice you can, at any given point in time.
> Whatever the outcome, you will handle it.

Find your answers in the information you have

Begin by finding (or creating) an interruption-free space where you have lots of room to spread things out around you. Sit at a large desk or table. You will need the book, journal or document in which you have captured all of your responses from the exercises (or a hard copy of your electronic notes), a pen, a vivid marker and a supply of A4-sized paper (either blank or lined).

Using the vivid marker, head up a new piece of paper for each of your life areas, just as you did initially when you set up the template in which you have recorded some of your responses. I suggest you use a vivid marker, so that you can easily distinguish each life-area page from the others.

Visual people tend to prefer this paper-based approach.

However, you can just as easily create an electronic template, if you prefer. Simply open a new document and use your life areas as page headings.

Once you have created a new template (using whichever medium works best for you), I want you to focus on one life area at a time. Keeping your thoughts focused on just one life area will allow you to develop a clearer 'picture' of what you want that particular aspect of your life to include.

Choose which life area you will begin with.

Now take your time and work through all of the information you have gathered from completing the exercises in the preceding chapters which relate to that particular life area. This will involve the following.

1. Reviewing all of the non-life-area-specific thoughts you recorded, to identify which ideas and comments are relevant to the life area you are focusing on. This will include your responses to the 'Get to know yourself' exercises (Chapter 8).

    Look at what you learned about yourself in Chapter 8. Consider each insight you gained in response to the 'Get to know yourself' questions: How might each insight apply to this life area? And in what way? What are the future implications of what you now know about yourself? Of the things that you enjoy, which relate to this life area? In what ways could you up your game in this area of your life?

2. Reviewing the responses you recorded on the template for this life area. This will include your life-area-specific responses to:

   › the values exercise (Chapter 9)

   › the passions exercise (Chapter 10)

> the three 'what' questions and the prompt
questions exercises (Chapter 11).

As you review your life-area-specific responses, which
ideas or thoughts resonate most with you? Which
excite you — or perhaps excite and scare you at the
same time?

Begin creating your shortlist

You are looking for what I call the 'gems' in the information
you have. These include the thoughts or ideas that jump out
at you, stir a reaction within you, or simply make you smile
at the possibilities they hold. Continually ask yourself,
'What do I want for myself in terms of ... (the life area you
are focusing on)?'

In Chapter 5 we discussed the importance of ensuring
that what we do, and what we choose for our lives, are
important and meaningful to us, in order for us to be
sustainably happy. Stay focused on what truly matters to
you. Don't allow yourself to be distracted by the volume
of information you have in front of you — look for what
matters most to you and feels most right with respect to the
area of your life you are focusing on.

Transfer (from your original life-area workings) or add
your gems to your newly headed page for the life area
on which you are focusing. This is the beginning of the
shortlist of what you most want for this area of your life.
You will have the opportunity later to further refine this
list, so it needn't be perfect at this stage, but certainly aim
for a very close representation of what you want for yourself
with respect to this life area.

Get specific!

Keep drilling down into the information you have. Keep digging. Continually ask yourself, 'What do I want?' Seek to understand yourself and your responses completely. And always strive to be as specific as you can. Be your own life coach and keep asking yourself relevant questions that make you drill down further and further into the specifics of what you are thinking about.

Let's take an example so you can see what I mean. Meet Christine. She is passionate about dancing. She loves to dance and feels completely in her element when she is on the floor. Recently made redundant from her job, Christine sought coaching to help her clarify what was next for her, career-wise.

Several of her family members and close friends kept telling her to use her redundancy payout to set up her own dance school. She didn't know what to do. She felt stuck, uncertain about her future, and confused. While she loved dancing, she didn't share others' enthusiasm for the idea of her teaching, yet she couldn't understand why she felt that way. She started to think that maybe she *should* teach. Perhaps her friends were right? After all, dancing is what she loves, and what she's good at.

As part of a wider exercise to help understand her values and passions, I encouraged Christine to talk to me about her passion for dancing. I kept asking questions, encouraging her to be as specific as she could. 'What do you most love about your dancing?' 'What are you doing when you experience most deeply that feeling of "complete joy"' you speak of?'

As we drilled down and became increasingly specific about the nature of her passion, Christine realised that her passion for dancing was about performing to her best ability, about being as competitive as she could. No wonder she had little or no interest in teaching dance. Teaching others how to dance wasn't her passion.

Christine's passion was about her own dancing — she trained hard to be as good as she could be, and enjoyed the satisfaction of doing well at competitions. Suddenly Christine could see why she had felt so lukewarm about others' suggestion that she should teach. While she was undoubtedly passionate about dancing, it was understanding the specific nature of that passion that allowed Christine to confidently make a decision that this particular passion wasn't one she wanted to pursue as her next career move.

Christine's example demonstrates how important it is to be as specific as you can about what it is that you think and feel. The reality is that Christine would be as well suited to teaching dancing as her rugby-playing teenage son. Don't stop at knowing what you love to do: seek to understand what it is about those things that you most enjoy. Don't be content to know what you are good at: seek to pinpoint the exact nature of your most valuable skills or talents, and to understand in what environments you most enjoy and are most effective in using them.

I wholeheartedly believe that we all have the answers within us. In order to be able to access those answers you need to keep asking yourself questions — questions that will allow you to get to the specifics you need in order to make the best possible decisions.

Identify your gaps

As a coach, I help people close the gap between where they are now and where they want to be. I encourage you to identify your gaps.

In which of your life areas is there currently the biggest gap between where you are now and where you want to be in terms of your level of happiness and contentment? What is currently in this gap? In other words, what is missing? How can you close this gap? What does your ideal solution look like? What action could you take?

Common gaps and goal areas

The list below includes the areas in which people most commonly choose to set goals. Which, if any, of these jump out as being most relevant for you? What items, for you, are missing from this list?

Health and well-being/fitness

> Increase fitness.

> Increase energy levels.

> Improve health — generally or in relation to a specific issue.

> Reduce stress.

> Complete a significant organised event, such as a marathon, triathlon, ironman.

> Strengthen self-esteem.

Knowledge and learning

> Study / achieve higher qualifications.

> Learn a new skill or hobby.

Time for self/self-care

> Complete a creative project.

> Try something new that you've always wanted to do.

Finances

> Become debt-free.

> Save money.

Romance and significant other
> Start a new relationship.

> Improve or enhance an existing relationship.

> End a relationship that is no longer working.

Friends
> Develop new friendships.

> Improve or enhance existing friendships.

> End friendships that are no longer working.

Family
> Improve existing relationships.

> Spend more time with those who matter most to you.

Physical environment
> Improve or completely change your living and/or work environments so that they 'feed' you.

Career
> Find a new job.

> Aim for a promotion.

> Start a new business.

> Grow an existing business.

> Improve personal productivity.

Do not restrict yourself to the goal areas included here. This list is provided only as an ideas list. It is by no means exhaustive. Also note that the life areas 'Community' and 'Spirituality' are not included above. Take the time to consider each of these life areas as well. Is there a gap between where you are and where you want to be, with respect to these life areas? If so, identify the specific nature of that gap. Understanding your gaps will help you identify possible goals.

Recognise your 'big goal' opportunities

You will recall my discussion of the power of big goals. Big goals are those that stretch us, that take us outside our comfort zones and that sometimes have us achieve things we never thought possible. Big goals both excite and scare us. Not surprisingly, they also tend to be life-changing.

Looking at the information you have in front of you, what is the one change you could make, the one big goal you could go after, that would have the biggest positive impact on your life at this point?

Do the research

If you struggle to be clear about what you want with respect to any aspect(s) of your life, think about what additional information might help you.

If you are looking at various career options, but can't decide which one to pursue, talk to people who are already in those roles. The internet is another useful source of information. Find out more about what is actually involved, gain a more detailed understanding of the various options you are considering, until you have sufficient information to allow a preference to emerge.

If you want to widen your circle of friends, find out what groups and organisations there are in your community. You could start by visiting your local information or advice centre, looking online or simply talking to other people.

Rather than saying, 'but I still don't know', ask yourself, 'What information do I need that will enable me to know?' and 'Where will I find that information?' Apply the same drill-down principle as before and keep digging until you have sufficient knowledge to enable you to decide what you most want.

When I first set out to clarify what I wanted to do career-wise, at the point when I finally realised my strategy of waiting for my dream job to find me wasn't working, I had never heard of 'life coaching'. I didn't know what I wanted to do. I was clear, however, that I wanted to work with people. To help, inspire and educate others, and to do so in an area or a way in which I could make a real difference. I didn't see myself as a counsellor, a psychologist or a trainer, and yet there were aspects of each of these roles that really appealed.

So what did I do? I listed the aspects of those three jobs that most appealed to me. And I went online. With the help of Google I spent many (and I stress, *many*) hours looking at what others working in the areas of counselling, psychology, and training were doing. I looked at combinations of those roles, and at the specific aspects I had included on my list. After plenty of reading, many dead-ends, and more than a few disheartening sighs (wondering if I would ever find the work I was meant to do), my search introduced me to the field of coaching.

The more I understood about the coaching approach and its philosophy, the more excited I became. I then identified ten well-established life coaches and set about contacting them. Over the course of a couple of days I interviewed all ten. It was an incredibly uplifting and vital part of my research. Thanks to the wonderful generosity of those I contacted, I was able, reasonably quickly, to gain a greater knowledge of what the reality of working as a coach would entail and to have my 101 questions answered.

I specifically sought advice on the various training options available. This enabled me to identify my preferred provider quickly. To gain hands-on experience, I also started working with a life coach myself as a client. After all, what better way to fully understand what the job entails than to experience the benefits yourself?

I share my own experience with you to reinforce the importance of doing the research. Yes, it is time consuming. And initially, at least, it can be challenging — especially if at the outset you have few clues about where to begin. The key, however, is to keep digging. We are fortunate in this age of the internet to have so much information readily accessible. Use it. Believe that the information you seek is there somewhere and do the work (research) to find it. Get online. Read. Talk to people. Do whatever it takes.

Accept that it may feel hard … you are probably out of practice

With so much information to work through, so many options to consider and factors to think about, I know that this whole process can feel somewhat daunting. That's okay. I am asking you to decide what you want — something that most people are completely unused to doing.

Think about it. Sure, we each make day-to-day decisions, but even these tend to be influenced by others, often a boss or significant others. We tend to follow similar routines, to go to the same places, and have the same conversations with the same people, about the same things. Much of our lives is more reflective of our daily habits than of our ability to make decisions.

It is no wonder, therefore, that working through a process that requires you to know what you want may feel challenging. You are being asked to do something that is relatively unfamiliar to you. Once you understand this, I hope you will be able to acknowledge any unease, recognise it for what it is, and continue to work through this process with self-confidence. Just because you may be out of practice at knowing what you want, doesn't mean you *can't* know what you want.

Stay solution-focused

If you feel stuck during the course of deciding what you want, figure out what you need to do in order to become unstuck — then do it. Consider what you most need at this time. Chances are, it will be one of the following:

> more information: do the research

> more courage: act despite your fear

> more faith in yourself: trust your ability to make the best decision you can at this time.

Stay solution-focused. That is, stay completely focused on being able to decide what you want for yourself. Don't allow 'I don't know' to be your answer. Keep asking yourself questions and looking for ideas and solutions, until you do know. Remember that in order for you to know what you want, you have to decide what you want. No one else can do this for you ... so keep going.

Eliminate any 'shoulds'

It matters that what you identify as wanting in your life is strictly what *you* want. Keep checking your ideas and thoughts and eliminate any items that are 'shoulds'. 'Shoulds' are those items that at some level you feel as though you should want, and yet, in your gut, you know they are not an absolute reflection of what you personally desire.

Our 'shoulds' tend to be things that our parents or those closest to us think we should do. These things are often accompanied by a sense of obligation or 'heaviness' when we think about them.

If there is an item on your list that isn't completely, absolutely, undeniably what *you* want for yourself, do yourself the favour of removing it. Your life is *your* life, no one else's. This is an exercise about you deciding what you want in life, not what others want for you.

If all else fails, clear out the cupboards

That's right. If, despite applying yourself wholeheartedly to the task of deciding what you want, you are still not sure, grant yourself permission to organise an aspect of your physical environment. Remember how great it felt the last time you cleared out your wardrobe and got rid of those clothes you hadn't worn for years? Recall how energised and light you always feel after de-cluttering the garage or organising your office space? It's a well-known fact that the state of your physical environment can have a dramatic impact on how you feel about yourself.

If all else fails, choose an aspect of your environment that needs sorting, and get into action. While on one level this may seem a distraction from the greater task at hand of clarifying what you want in life, you may actually find that the boost in how you feel will provide the very shift in energy and perspective you needed. And, as a bonus, your home or office will get an unexpected spring clean.

Your 'what I want' shortlist

Once you have reviewed all of your answers to the previous exercises, considered all of the information you now have at your disposal and made some decisions between the various ideas and options you identified, you will have a shortlist of what you want, with respect to each of your life areas.

Look at the answers you have come to.

> How do you feel about your list?

> ❭ What aspects are certainties as opposed to aspects you are less sure about?

> ❭ What aspects feel right as opposed to not-so-right?

> ❭ Do the items on your shortlist honour and express your values? Are there any aspects that seem inconsistent with your values?

> ❭ Are your passions adequately reflected in your shortlisted items?

For those aspects that don't feel quite right, put some effort into understanding why. Consider these questions:

> ❭ What is missing here?

> ❭ What else might you choose instead?

> ❭ What would you choose to do (with respect to this area of your life) if you knew you couldn't fail?

> ❭ What do you really, really want?

From shortlist to master list

Keep working on your shortlist until you are completely happy with it.

How do you feel about your list now? Are you confident that it fully reflects what you most want in life? How does the thought of living your list make you feel?

At the point where your list feels right, where you feel it accurately reflects what you most want for yourself, make it your master list. The items on your master list should completely excite and inspire you, yet also make you feel nervous. Trust that you will know when your list is right for you.

Still stuck, unsure what you want?

Still feeling stuck, unsure what you want for yourself? Please do not read beyond this chapter until you have done the work required, and have decided what you want for yourself. Don't tell yourself 'I'll come back to it later', because chances are you won't. We both know that. Don't accept 'I just don't know' as being good enough. If you are still not sure what you want, go back to the beginning of Chapter 8 and work your way through the process again. Reflect more deeply, ask yourself more questions, take your time to do more research — do whatever you need to do to arrive at the position of knowing what you want. We talked about taking personal responsibility in Chapter 3. This is your opportunity to take responsibility for knowing what you want. The answers are within the information you now have. Allow yourself to find them.

13

Set seriously fabulous goals

'This one step, choosing a goal and sticking to it, changes everything.'

— Scott Reed

'A life without goals is like a race without a finish line.'

— Author unknown

Once you are clear about what you want for yourself, once you are happy with your master list, it is vital that you turn these ideas and dreams into specific, concrete, written goals.

The importance of goals

Living without clear goals is like driving a car in torrential rain. No matter how powerful or well-maintained your car, you drive slowly, hesitantly, taking extra care and prolonging your journey.

Deciding on your goals stops the rain and enables you to focus your energies and abilities on what you really want. It enables you to take control of your life and achieve what you want.

Goal setting 101

Much has been written about goal setting and goal getting — and I certainly don't claim to be espousing anything new. But I do want to reiterate the key facts about goal setting. Goal setting is an incredibly powerful tool and one that shouldn't be underestimated. If you are serious about being successful and living a kick-arse life, great goal setting is imperative.

What we can learn from successful people

There are many books describing the secrets of success, the strategies and behaviours of people who have become highly successful. I want to briefly share some of these with you. We can learn a lot from those who are already living extraordinary lives.

Write down your goals

Successful people recognise the power of writing their goals down. This may sound simplistic but I can personally attest to the difference between having a goal and having a written goal.

There was a famous study conducted in 1953 in which graduating seniors of a major university were asked whether they had written goals, and plans to achieve them after they left university.

Brian Tracy suggests that the simple act of writing your goals down increases your chance of success by at least 1000 per cent.

Of the respondents, only 3 per cent had written goals and plans. Twenty years later, in 1973, the researchers re-contacted those same graduates. They asked them, among other things, about their financial status. They found that the 3 per cent of students who had had clear, written goals at the time of graduation were now worth more, in financial terms, than the entire other 97 per cent of graduates put together.

In response to this result, the Harvard Business School conducted a similar study between 1979 and 1989. Students who were graduating from the MBA programme at Harvard were asked the same question: 'Have you set clear, written goals for your future and made plans to accomplish them?' The results were identical. Three per cent of the graduating students had written goals. In addition, 14 per cent had goals, but they were not in writing. The other 83 per cent reported having no clear goals.

A decade later, in 1989, the researchers interviewed those same graduates again. Those students who had goals that were not written down were earning on average twice as much as the 83 per cent who had left university with no clear goals. However, most remarkable was the finding that the 3 per cent of students who had started off with clear, written goals and plans, were now earning on average ten times as much as the other 97 per cent put together.

Why does the act of writing down a goal have such a powerful impact? Writing down a goal gives it life and energy. A goal that isn't in writing is merely a wish or a fantasy. Put it in writing and you give it power. You begin to think about what it will feel like and look like to have achieved your goal. You begin to see that your goal is much more than just words. And this is what you want to happen. As you allow yourself to truly connect with how you will feel and what it will be like when you have achieved your goal, this serves to increase your desire. Your goal becomes more real. And in turn, you begin to desire it even more.

The power of desire

You want your desire for your goal to be nothing short of consuming and obsessive. You want to have a burning, unfailing desire. Why? Because you want your desire to be so strong and magnetic that you can't imagine not-achieving your goal. It will be this passion and desire that helps you get out of bed every morning, desiring to move another step closer to your goal. It will be these feelings that allow you to maintain your focus and drive, even in the face of setbacks or issues.

From ideas to great goals

Assuming you have successfully completed the exercises in the preceding chapters, you will have a list of things you want in your life, your master list. Ideas are a great starting point. The next step is to transform these ideas into goals. Goals are very specific and significantly more powerful than ideas.

Paul Meyer's SMART acronym has become synonymous with goal-setting literature. Goals that are SMART (Specific, Measurable, Achievable, Realistic and Time-bound) are more likely to be achieved.

Let's take a closer look at each of these characteristics.

Specific   Great goals are well-defined and focused. To be specific, you need to first consider the six 'W's' — who, what, where, when, which and why. 'Lose 10 kg by 31 March by working with a personal trainer and attending at least four group fitness classes each week' is a far more specific goal than 'lose weight'. You can see how a specific goal involves far more planning and thought than a more general goal.

Measurable   It is important to establish concrete criteria or milestones against which you can track your progress toward achieving your goal. This will help you stay on track, and maintain your motivation. There is nothing like seeing progress toward achieving your end goal to spur you on.

A goal without a measurable outcome is like a sports competition without a scoreboard or a scorekeeper. How would you know who has won? Or, in the context of goal setting, how will you know when you have achieved your goal? With any goal it is vital for you to be able to measure when it has been achieved. An effective goal statement should always answer the question, 'how much or how many?' Taking our goal example, 'lose 10 kg by 31 March by working with a personal trainer and attending at least four group fitness classes each week', the measurable aspect of this (i.e. the answer to the question 'how much or how many?') is '10 kg'.

Achievable   A goal can only be achieved if it is achievable. While I advocate setting goals that stretch you, your goals need to be possible to attain. Be clear about the resources your goal will require, including attitudinal resources, skills, abilities and financial resources. There is no benefit in setting a goal that is simply unachievable. 'Lose 10 kg by the end of next week ...' would be one such example.

Realistic   Make sure that each goal is consistent with other goals you have established and fits in with your immediate or long-term plans. For example, someone who has a newborn baby, is keen to return to full-time study, has always wanted to write a book, and is contemplating training for their first marathon would need to think very carefully about whether taking on all of the above at one time is realistic. What is realistic for one person may be completely unrealistic for another. Whether a goal is realistic is often a personal judgement call that only you can make. Only you know what is realistic for you.

Time-bound   A goal should have a time frame by which it will be achieved. Without a time frame there is no sense of urgency. Which is more likely to spur you into action, 'Lose 10 kg' or 'Lose 10 kg by 31 March'? Time frames are motivating.

Turn your ideas into goals

Now it is time for you to turn your list of goal ideas or intentions into effective goal statements. Use the SMART characteristics to help you with this. For each of your goals, ask yourself:

> Is it specific?

> Is it measureable?

> Is it achievable?

> Is it realistic?

> Is it time-bound?

The following list provides examples of SMART goals. Looking at examples of other people's goals can be a useful way to get your own creative juices flowing.

Health and well-being/fitness

> To weigh 85 kg by ... (specific date)

> To stop smoking by ... (specific date)

> To complete the New York Marathon on ... (specific date)

> To do three yoga classes per week starting on ... (specific date)

Knowledge and learning

› To have completed a PhD in Psychology by …(specific date)

› To be an active member of the local Toast Masters Association by … (specific date)

› To speak French fluently by … (specific date)

› To have been to France and Italy by … (specific date)

Time for self/self-care

› To meditate daily starting … (specific date — today's date!)

› To have my first book published by … (specific date)

Finances

› To have zero credit card debt by … (specific date)

› To be mortgage-free by … (specific date)

› To have saved $10,000 by … (specific date)

› To be a millionaire by … (specific date)

Romance and significant other

› To be in a fantastic new relationship by … (specific date)

› To have a weekly 'date' with my partner, starting … (specific date — today's date!)

› To have planned a holiday together, just the two of us, by … (specific date)

› To end my existing relationship by … (specific date)

Friends

› To develop … (state a number) new friendships by … (specific date)

› To strengthen my friendship with … (name(s)) by … (specific date)

> To end my friendship with ... (name) by ... (specific date)

Family

> To strengthen my relationship with ... (name(s)) by ... (specific date)

> To do at least three fun things with my children each day, starting ... (specific date — today's date!)

Physical environment

> To be living on a lifestyle property by ... (specific date)

> To have fully renovated my home by ... (specific date)

> To be living/working in ... (state other city or country) by ... (specific date)

> To have created a home studio that I love by ... (specific date)

Career

> To find a new job I love by ... (specific date)

> To start my own business by ... (specific date)

> To increase my business' profitability to ... (state figure) by ... (specific date)

> To be earning ... (state a figure) a month in passive income by ... (specific date)

Keep 'fine-tuning' your goal statements until you are completely satisfied with them.

The 'excited yet nervous' test

How do you feel about your goals? Do they excite you? Do they make you feel a tad nervous? If the answer to both of these is 'yes', that's perfect!

Do you remember that I talked earlier about

It makes sense that your goals excite you. If they are indeed what you really, really want for yourself, then the thought of being able to achieve them should energise you.

145

Your goals should both excite you and make you feel nervous. This is a good indicator that your goals are sufficiently big. Living a 'kick-arse life' isn't about having small, easy-to-achieve goals. It's about stretching yourself.

having a burning desire for your goals? It is the degree of this desire, the extent to which your goals excite you, that will keep you motivated and taking action towards achieving them. If your goals don't excite you, you may as well cross them off your list right now. Goals that feel like a chore, or leave you with a heavy heart are never going to inspire you into action. Make sure your goals excite you — the more, the better.

Stay focused on what you want

Once your goals have been finalised, dwell on them constantly.

*'You become what you think about
most of the time.'*

— Brian Tracy

Focus your time and attention on what you want. It's what successful people do.

There has been much research on success and the characteristics and behaviours of successful people. When asked what they think about most of the time, successful people say that they tend to spend most of their time focusing on what they want, and how they are going to get it.

In contrast, unsuccessful, unhappy people tend to think about what they don't want. They talk about what they don't want in their life, what's not working for them, or about who is to blame for how they are currently feeling.

Don't underestimate the power of thought. Successful people know they will achieve their goals. They don't just hope or desire to, they absolutely know and believe they will be successful and will achieve what they want. And so they do. They visualise having achieved their goals. They can see what success will look like. They know how they will feel. The more they focus on what they want, the closer they move towards realising that goal.

'Whatever we plant in our subconscious mind and nourish with repetition and emotion will one day become a reality.'

— Earl Nightingale

How does this work? The key here is understanding that your subconscious mind doesn't distinguish between what 'is' and what 'is yet to be'. As you focus on your goals, you impress them deeper and deeper into your subconscious mind. As time passes, your subconscious mind will accept your goals as directives from your conscious mind. You will start to see your actions and words fitting a pattern consistent with your goals. You will start to see opportunities present themselves that will move you closer to achieving your goals.

'Whatever the mind can conceive and believe, it can achieve.'

— Napoleon Hill

Focus on your goals, daily. Visualise them, as though you have already achieved them. The following two exercises are specifically designed to help you do so.

Bring your goals to life

This exercise will help you to create a mental picture of how your life will be different and how you will feel, once you have achieved each of your key goals. It will allow you to bring your goals to life.

Take the time to write a list of at least 20 things that will be different in your life once you have achieved each of your goals. Write a separate list with respect to each goal.

This exercise may take some time. Keep going until you have identified at least 20 items for each goal. Don't stop until you have identified at least 20 ways in which your life will be different. If you can think of more than 20, by all means keep adding to your list until you feel it is complete.

From now on, as you focus on each goal, daily, hopefully the emotions and thoughts identified in completing this exercise will serve to further feed your excitement and drive to achieve your goals.

Create a visual representation of your goals

When I work with clients who are clearly very visual, I encourage them to create a collage of images that represent their various goals. These are often called vision boards. If this is a new idea to you, I encourage you to look online to see examples of what others have created. Simply search 'vision board' in Google Images. I hope it will inspire you into action.

This is something I have personally found to be incredibly valuable. Every image is hand picked to represent a particular goal or feeling (i.e. how you will feel having achieved a particular goal). It becomes a very personal, very clear representation of what you most want in your life.

If you are also a visual person, you will already appreciate how powerful the right picture can be. Why not create your own masterpiece? Keep it where you can see it often. Just looking at your collage will excite you. You will be amazed how energised and motivated it will make you feel.

Reflective questions

SET SERIOUSLY FABULOUS GOALS

What one goal excites you the most? Why?

What one goal, once achieved, will have the most significant impact on your life?

What else do you want? (Is there anything missing from your goals?)

How do you feel about what is ahead for you?

14

Make it happen

*'It is not what you say, or wish,
or hope or intend, it is only
what you do that counts.'*

— Brian Tracy

'Five frogs are sitting on a log. Four decide to jump off. How many are left? The answer: five. Because there's a difference between deciding and doing.' This frequently quoted saying of Mark L. Feldman and Michael F. Spratt's makes an incredibly important distinction between intention and action.

It is one thing to decide to do something, but that decision is meaningless unless you act on it.

If you have successfully completed the exercises in this book you will know what you want for yourself, or at least be a lot closer to that point. Now is the time to act on your goals.

Create an action plan

Goals, particularly goals that stretch you, can seem rather daunting. Until, that is, you break them down into smaller, more manageable, bite-size action steps.

As the old proverb says: 'How do you eat an elephant?' The answer? 'One mouthful at a time.'

> *'If you really want something*
> *you can figure out how to make it happen.'*
>
> — M. C. Escher

Look at your immediate goals, and for each one, list all of the things you need to do, the specific, tangible actions you need to take to make your goal a reality.

Consider:

> ❭ What do you need to do to get from here to there?
>
> ❭ What needs to happen for you to achieve this goal?
>
> ❭ Whom else do you need to involve/contact to make this happen?

Write down everything that comes to mind.

Once you have listed everything you can think of (and be open to coming back to your list and adding more actions as they come to mind), put the items into sequential order. Consider: What needs to happen first? What needs to happen next? And then what?

Keep going until you are comfortable with the action plan in front of you. The exercise of preparing an action plan may be relatively straightforward for some goals. However, for others, it may require you to do some research first so that you can identify the various steps and actions required. You may want to contact others who have already achieved a similar goal, or you may benefit from undertaking online research.

Remember, we 'don't know what we don't know until we know it' (a phrase I frequently use), so don't be afraid to ask others for help as you prepare your action plan. Who will be able to help you? This may or may not be someone you already know.

The following list provides examples of possible actions with respect to each goal area. These may provide a useful starting point from which you can identify your own action steps, the nature of which will, of course, depend on the specific nature of your goals.

Health and well-being/fitness

> Have a full medical examination.
> Start working with a personal trainer at your local gym.
> Find out what sports events are coming up and register for one of them.
> Increase the number of hours' sleep you are currently getting.
> Analyse your nutrition — record your food intake over the course of a week. What does this show you? What healthier choices will you make?
> Seek professional advice from a nutritionist.
> Join a gym.
> Go online or visit your local library or bookshop to research the particular aspect of health and well-being or fitness that is most relevant to your goal.
> Start keeping a gratitude diary — each night just before you go to bed, write down at least five things you are grateful for, from your day.
> Find out what sporting clubs and other organisations exist in your area — assess which ones are most relevant to your goal, and join.

> Make a list of at least 30 things you are currently tolerating in your life that cause you stress or angst and start eliminating or handling these — one per day.

Knowledge and learning

> Go online or to your local library or training institution and find out about classes or courses that interest you (these might include night class, one-off courses or degree courses). Remember to also consider distance-learning options.

Time for self/self-care

> Go online or undertake appropriate research to find out more about interests or passions you wish to further develop, or things you have always wanted to do. Find out specifically what's involved.

> Refer back to the 'Things I enjoy' list you were encouraged to write in Chapter 8 and increase the number of items from the list that you are doing per day.

Finances

> Analyse your current financial situation — track your spending over the period of a month. Pinpoint how you are currently spending your money. What does this show you? Use this information to prepare a budget.

> Seek financial advice from a financial consultant or professional.

> Go online or visit your local library or bookshop to learn more about financial options.

> Remove your credit cards from your wallet.

> Talk to your current bank, and others, to see what products they offer.

> Brainstorm ways in which you can increase your personal and/or household income.

> Study those who are already financially successful to learn how they achieved their success in this area.

Romance and significant other

Start a new relationship

> Make a list of at least 25 qualities or characteristics you want in a partner.

> Make a list of at least 10 places where you might meet the type of partner you want.

> Find out about groups, clubs and organisations in your local area that interest you and that could potentially provide the opportunity for you to meet a new partner.

> Register with reputable online dating agencies.

> Talk to people you know who are in relationships and find out how and where they met their partners.

> Let your friends and family know you are ready to meet someone new so they, too, can help with your search.

Improve an existing relationship

> Write a list of 15 things about your partner that first attracted you to them.

> Write a list of at least 10 things you used to both enjoy doing together. Which of these (if any) would you like to do together again?

> See a relationship counsellor.

> Plan a holiday together.

> Make spending regular time together, having fun, a priority.

> Set joint goals and achieve them, together.

End a relationship that is no longer working

> Consider the various ways and options around how you can end the relationship, and choose the one that is most respectful for both of you.

> Write a list of the reasons why you are choosing to no longer be in the relationship (remember to take responsibility for your part in the relationship ending). This will help you clarify your thoughts and thus allow you to communicate more succinctly and effectively.

> See a grief counsellor (grief counsellors help those experiencing any form of loss, including the ending of a relationship).

> Following the break-up, write a letter to your ex-partner saying anything that you feel has been left unsaid. Remember, too, to thank him or her for the many positive things you gained from the relationship (listing them). Once you have written it, *do not* give the letter to your ex-partner. Destroy it.

Friends

Develop new friendships

> Make a list of at least 10 places where you might meet new friends. Think about what you would most like to have in common with your friends. How does this influence where you might meet such people?

> Find out about groups, clubs and organisations in your local area that interest you and that could potentially provide the opportunity for you to meet new friends.

> Explore online opportunities for meeting others who have the same interests as you do (social media, blogging sites, etc.).

> Host a party or get-together, asking everyone to bring along someone new.

Improve existing friendships

> Make joint plans to do more fun things together, and brainstorm ideas. Don't be afraid to be outright silly!

> Make a conscious effort to be 'fully present' when with your friends.

End friendships that no are no longer working

> Consider the various ways you might end the friendship, and choose the option that is most respectful for both of you.

Family

> Make a list of at least 30 fun things you could do as a family. Why not involve the whole family in this exercise?
> Plan a family holiday.
> Look at your weekly routine and identify opportunities to increase the amount of quality time you spend together as a family.

Physical environment

> Make a list of aspects of your current environment that you are tolerating or 'putting up with' and start eliminating these, one by one.
> Approach a real estate agent to give you a market appraisal on your property.
> Make a list, collect images, start collating a file of ideas on what your 'ideal' environment will include (to clarify what your renovations or new house will look like).

Career

Find a new job

> Go online and research your dream job. Identify others already successful in that field and contact them. Find out what training or skills you need to enter the field. Identify the best possible way of transitioning into your dream job.

> Brainstorm ways in which you could achieve your dream job — list at least 10 ideas.
> Enrol in any required training/course.
> Update your CV.
> Hone your job-interview skills (there are plenty of great resources available online).
> Meet with recruitment consultants who specialise in your chosen industry/field.

Start a new business

> Write a business plan for your business concept. If initially this seems too 'hard', begin by writing a one-pager setting out your business concept. This can become the basis of your business plan once you have more information.
> Write a marketing plan. Begin by clearly describing your product or service, identify your key competitors and the points of difference between their product or service and yours, assess the demand for what you are offering and outline your pricing strategy. Then itemise your marketing budget and identify the specific advertising and promotional actions you will take to market your business. Templates are available online to help you write your marketing plan.
> Write a list of all of the things you need in order to start your own business.
> Write a separate list of any new skills you will need to gain or strengthen in order to start your own business.
> List any additional skills you will require that you could hire-in or outsource. (Finances, marketing, graphic design and technology support are skills commonly hired-in.)
> Go online to research or visit your key potential competitors to further develop your business concept and to help you refine your point-of-difference.

> Go online or visit your local library or bookshop and research the fundamentals of new business success.

> Make a list of possible investors for your business.

> Identify what new business support is available to you. What funding, support, educational and networking opportunities exist? (Locally based, industry-specific and online.)

> Meet with your lawyer, accountant and/or Inland Revenue to ensure you are fully aware of the legal obligations associated with setting up and running your own business.

Grow an existing business

> Complete a current profit-and-loss statement for your business. What does this show? What changes will you make as a result?

> Survey your existing customers to identify opportunities to further enhance your business.

> Complete a SWOT (strengths, weaknesses, opportunities, threats) analysis of your business. This involves undertaking an honest assessment of your business's internal strengths and weaknesses, and identifying current external opportunities and threats (risks).

> Make a list of potential new clients for your existing business, and plan how you are going to reach them.

> Update your marketing plan.

Consider who you need to be in order to live your plan

This may well seem a strange question, but think about it. You now have a clear set of goals and know what you need to do in order to achieve those goals. The 'what' is clear. But who do you need to be in order to be able to put your plan into action? What attributes will be most advantageous, given your goals?

Who you need to be

Complete this sentence:

'In order to achieve my goals I need to be someone who ...'

. . . is organised?

. . . isn't afraid to ask for help?

. . . no longer accepts less than what I know I can have?

. . . is patient with myself?

. . . takes good care of myself?

. . . will say 'no' more often?

. . . is determined?

You may have several answers. That's fine. At least one of these is likely to be an attribute or a 'something' that doesn't come naturally to you. Once you have your answer(s), consider what this will mean for you in practical terms.

For example, if, given the extent of the changes you wish to make, you identify that from now on you need to be someone who takes better care of yourself, consider how you can begin to do this. What self-care action(s) can you start taking today? What self-care practices can you start to incorporate into your new daily routine? If, in order to achieve your goals, you identify that you need to be someone who can say 'no' more often, practise doing so, effective immediately. The more you say 'no', the easier and more comfortable it will become. Bear in mind that those around may be somewhat surprised as you begin to say 'no'. They may react. Don't be put off by this. Remind yourself that saying 'no' will free up more time for you, time you can use to move closer to achieving your goals.

Act on your action plan

While planning is important, make sure it is followed by action. Your plan doesn't have to be perfect. It just needs to be good enough to get you into action. Don't allow yourself to spend too much time planning and thinking about what you need to do *instead of acting* on your plan.

> 'To think too long about doing a thing
> often becomes its undoing.'

> — Eva Young

This can be an easy trap to fall into; believe me, I know! For as long as I can remember, I have thought I would write a book one day, maybe even several. Three years ago I decided what this, my first book, would be about. I wrote an outline. I listed the key messages. I set myself a time frame. It felt good. I was finally about to write my book.

And then what did I do? Nothing. Not in relation to my book, anyway. Not until last year, when I finally realised that this book wasn't going to write itself. If I was going to get my message out to the world, I needed to overcome my 'but what if it's not good enough' and 'what if no one will publish it' fears and start typing. And here it is. Finally.

Planning is important but it won't in itself allow you to achieve your goals. Do the planning ... then act on your plan!

I don't have a way of knowing what the statistics would be for this, but I dare say a significant proportion of amazing ideas never get past the planning stage. How many books have been left partially written? How many fantastic new products never get past the idea stage? How many ingenious new services never get to be experienced?

I am reminded of what Nolan Bushnell has said: 'Everyone who's ever taken a shower has had an idea. It's the person who gets out of the shower, dries off and does something about it who makes a difference.' Imagine how different the world might be if every single idea ever conceived in the shower was acted on and came to fruition.

Think about it.

Now make a commitment, just as I did with respect to this book, that you *will* take the necessary actions to successfully achieve your goals.

If you struggle to complete an action plan, simply ask yourself, 'What is the first step?' And do it. Then ask yourself, 'Now what? What is the next step?' In other words, don't let your 'not knowing' (or fear) stop you from acting. Taking the first step will usually be the hardest — so just take it! Once you start, you'll find your next steps will become evident and you'll have momentum to help you stay in motion. It's often said that it is easier to *stay* in motion, than to *get* in motion.

As you progress through the steps of your action plan, enjoy being able to physically cross each item off your list. Crossing items off, one by one, will motivate and energise you. That said, it's likely that your action plan will evolve along the way. Often it's not until you are in action, that you come to fully realise the steps involved in a given task. Be flexible.

Desire versus feeling – keep firmly focused on what you desire

There will be days when you simply don't feel like taking action toward your goal. I encourage you to make the distinction between desire and feeling at such times — and to choose to keep your eyes firmly focused on what you desire.

In talking about desire versus feeling, I immediately think of my own experience with my running. When I was training for my marathon, I followed a set training programme, and kept to it, to the letter. I never missed a scheduled run. However, that's not to say I was never tempted!

I lost count of the number of times I woke to my 5 a.m. alarm, desperately wanting to simply turn over and go back to sleep. Why get out of my warm bed to go out into the cold morning air to run for hours on end? It was often the last thing I felt like doing! BUT I was firmly focused on my desire to successfully complete a marathon, and pretty soon I would get over myself, and get moving. Had I simply focused on how I was feeling at that time, I assure you, there wouldn't have been much training done!

Focusing on what you desire, rather than how you are feeling at the time, is a powerful strategy to achieving your goals.

To me, this is the key to self-discipline.

An action a day

Commit to taking at least one action a day that moves you closer to achieving what you most want. On days when you are busy with other things, the action might be as little as making a phone call or sending an email. The key here is to get into action and stay in action.

Hesitation and procrastination stop far too many people from achieving greatness. Don't let them stop you. Use your time well. Get into the habit of asking yourself, 'Is what I am doing right now moving me closer to my goals?'

Expect 'wobbles' and use them to your advantage

As you begin to make your goals happen, there will be times when you will get the 'wobbles'. That is, despite being genuinely excited and enthused about your goal, suddenly you will feel stuck and less sure of yourself. This is normal. It doesn't feel very nice, but it is a natural reaction to putting yourself out there. It is your brain's defence mechanism, designed to keep you safe. It can be confusing. On one level you are out there, going after what you want, yet on a different level your body is telling you to retreat. It sees your goal as a threat.

When this happens, the first and most important thing to do is to recognise the phenomenon and see it for what it is.

The second is to refocus on your goal and why you want it, remind yourself that you can handle anything, and take the next action. Use 'wobbles' as an opportunity to reaffirm your commitment to having what you want in life. Remind yourself that 'wobbles' will come and go, but that goals achieved will stay with you for life!

See the opportunity in everything

In life things don't always go according to plan or how we would choose. Sometimes things happen that are beyond our control. A door may close. If or when this happens you have a choice: you can either repeatedly keep trying to walk through it, despite the fact that it is closed (be prepared to get a sore head!), or look for the next opportunity. Sometimes you'll need to look for an alternative way to the other side of that door. Other times, you may need to simply change your direction slightly, and head towards a different door.

'Obstacles don't have to stop you. If you run into a wall, don't turn around and give up. Figure out how to climb it, go through it, or work around it.'

— Michael Jordan

See the opportunity in everything. A problem sets you back. An opportunity allows you to continue moving forward. Choose to keep moving forward.

Surround yourself with like-minded, 'kick-arse' people

Surround yourself with people who motivate you and inspire possibility. According to Jim Rohn, 'You are the average of the five people you spend the most time with.' It makes sense that the habits, attitudes and behaviours of the people you spend the most time with can rub off on you, so choose to spend time with those whom you respect and admire. Successful people look for relationships with smart and resourceful people who push them, challenge them and inspire them to be their best.

Consider those with whom you spend most of your time. Are you surrounding yourself with the best possible people to fuel your success? Do you have the support, motivation and inspiration to help you reach your goals? Do you have people around you whom you admire and who genuinely want you to succeed? If not, make a conscious decision to seek out and meet more like-minded people. Don't underestimate what a powerful difference this can make.

Keep stretching yourself

As you reach your goals, set new ones. Keep moving forward. Keep your foot firmly on that accelerator pedal.

Decide what you want, make it big, make it matter and make it happen. And once you have achieved a goal, decide what you want next, make it even bigger, make it matter and make it happen, too ... and keep going. Keep stretching yourself.

Remember, there are no limits for what you can accomplish except for the limits you place on yourself.

Final thoughts ...

You have been challenged around the notion of waiting to live. We have discussed the importance of acting despite fear and of taking responsibility for your life. You know you can handle anything and have been encouraged to choose to live a kick-arse life. That is, to clarify what you want, make it big, make it matter and make it happen. Hopefully you have chosen to work through the process I have shared with you in this book, and you now know what you want in life, and are in the process of making it happen.

Whether you are in action creating the life you want, or still in the process of deciding what it is that you want for yourself, remember that the encouragement and motivation offered in these pages remains available to you. When you feel stuck, or in need of a lift, reread the parts that have most energised and inspired you, and made you feel good. Reread those parts not simply to make yourself feel better, but so that you can get back into action, back to creating the life you want and deserve.

Let's end this Waiting Epidemic, one extraordinary, kick-arse life at a time.

Now, it's your turn.

What are you waiting for? Get on with it!

Reflective questions

MAKE IT HAPPEN

Of all of the messages in this book, which has had the most powerful impact on you? Why?

How will you positively change your life, as a result?

Recommended reading

The following books are among my personal favourites. Whether or not I have directly referred to them in my writing, I credit these works for inspiring, challenging and developing my thinking.

Branson, Richard, *Like a Virgin: Secrets they won't teach you at business school*. Penguin, 2012.

Brown, Brene, *Daring Greatly: How the courage to be vulnerable transforms the way we live, love, parent and lead*. Gotham Books, 2012.

Chapman, Gary, *The Five Languages of Love: The secret to love that lasts*. Northfield Publishing, 1995.

Gladwell, Malcolm, *Outliers: The story of success*. Little, Brown and Company, 2008.

Jeffers, Susan, *Feel the Fear and Do it Anyway*. Random House, 2007.

Meyer, Paul J., *Attitude is Everything: If you want to succeed above and beyond*. Meyer Resource Group, 2003.

Syed, Matthew, *Bounce: The myth of talent and the power of practice*. Fourth Estate, 2011.

Tracy, Brian, *Goals! How to Get Everything You Want — Faster than You Ever Thought Possible*. Berrett-Koehler, 2010.

Woodham, Kerre, *Short Fat Chick to Marathon Runner*. HarperCollins, 2008.

The Power of the Second Question

Finding simple truths for complex lives

CHRIS SKELLETT

Following the success of his best-selling book *When Happiness Is Not Enough*, popular psychologist Chris Skellett has written *The Power of the Second Question* to show how you can make your life better and happier by harnessing the power of personal reflection to capture the 'simple truths' about your world. Each concise chapter suggests ideas, gives examples and reviews the importance of personal insight and celebrating the 'aha' moments. You are then invited to reflect upon your own wisdom in key areas of your life and to consolidate what you have learned from life so far. At the end of the process, you will have developed a much broader appreciation of who you are and what you have learned along life's journey, enabling you to reset your life's compass and pursue a course of renewed purpose and meaning.

EXISLE
PUBLISHING